INTRODUCTION
TO PASCAL

INTRODUCTION
TO PASCAL

NEILL GRAHAM

WEST PUBLISHING COMPANY

St. Paul   New York   Los Angeles   San Francisco

COPYRIGHT © 1980
By WEST PUBLISHING CO.
   50 West Kellogg Boulevard
   P.O. Box 3526
   St. Paul, Minnesota 55165

Library of Congress Cataloging in Publication Data

Graham, Neill, 1941–
   Introduction to PASCAL.
   Includes index.
   1. PASCL (Computer program language) I. Title.

QA76.73.P35G72   001.64'24   80–11314
ISBN 0-8299-0334-8

4th Reprint—1982

CONTENTS

Preface   ix

Chapter 1
**COMPUTERS, PROGRAMS, AND PROGRAMMING
LANGUAGES   1**

Information, Data, and Binary Codes   1
Computer Hardware   4
Computer Software   6

Chapter 2
PASCAL: FIRST STEPS   10

Data Types   10
The *write* and *writeln* Statements   15
A Pascal Program   20
Arithmetic in Pascal   23

Chapter 3
USING MAIN MEMORY   28

Variables   28
Declarations   29
Assignment   32
Input   37
An Example Program   39
Constant Definitions   41

Chapter 4
MORE ABOUT EXPRESSIONS   44

Expressions with More Than One Operator   44
Boolean Expressions   48
Standard Functions   54

Chapter 5
REPETITION   59

The **for** Statement   59
The **while** Statement   65
The **repeat** Statement   68

Chapter 6
SELECTION   72

One-way Selection   72
Two-way Selection   73
Multiway Selection   78

Chapter 7
FUNCTIONS AND PROCEDURES   88

Functions   88
Procedures   93
The Scopes of Identifiers   96
Using Global Variables   102
Recursion   105

Chapter 8
SIMPLE DATA TYPES   110

Scalar Data Types   110
Subrange Types   118

Chapter 9
STRUCTURED TYPES: ARRAYS   121

One-dimensional Arrays   121
Using One-dimensional Arrays   125
The Change-making Program   135
Multidimensional Arrays   138

Chapter 10
SEARCHING AND SORTING 146

Searching 146
Sorting 154

Chapter 11
STRUCTURED TYPES: RECORDS 175

Record Definitions 175
Nested Records 178
Record Variants 182
The Scopes of Field Identifiers 184
Pointer Types 187

Chapter 12
STRUCTURED TYPES: FILES 199

Standard File-handling Procedures 200
The Classical File-update Problem 204
Textfiles 210
The Files *input* and *output* 213

Chapter 13
STRUCTURED TYPES: SETS 215

Set Declarations 215
Operations on Sets 216
Using Sets 219

Appendix 1:
Pascal Reserved Words 225

Appendix 2:
The **goto** Statement 227

Appendix 3:
Declarations Assumed in Text 233

For Further Reading 235

Index 237

PREFACE

The programming language Pascal was originally developed for teaching programming, with emphasis on the techniques known as structured programming. More recently, as programmers in business and industry have begun to discover the limitations of traditional programming languages such as COBOL and FORTRAN, interest in putting Pascal to work outside the classroom has increased. An important boost for Pascal has come from its widespread implementation on microcomputers. More and more, Pascal is becoming one of the standard languages that every programmer should know.

This text is suitable for either an introductory course in Pascal or an introduction-to-programming course using Pascal. No previous programming experience on the part of the students is assumed. (Students who have had previous programming experience should be able to cover the first four chapters quite rapidly.)

The book starts out with an introductory chapter on information processing, computers, programs, programming languages, hardware, and software. The term "Pascal machine" is introduced for the combination of hardware and software that accepts and executes Pascal programs.

The study of Pascal itself begins with the second chapter, which introduces the standard data types, statements using the procedures *write* and *writeln* (which at this point are just called the *write* and *writeln* statements), and simple arithmetic expressions. Complete (although simple) Pascal programs are introduced at this point.

The next two chapters focus on subjects that are often troublesome to beginners—variables, assignment, arithmetic and Boolean expressions, and standard functions. All too many texts pass over these matters so quickly as to confuse beginners, particularly those without extensive mathematical backgrounds.

In chapter 5 we turn to the control mechanisms of Pascal—repetition, selection, functions, and procedures. Repetition is taken up before selection so as to get into realistic examples as soon as possible. Without repetition, it is difficult to find examples for which the use of a computer is justified.

Beginning with chapter 8, the emphasis shifts from control structures to data structures. User-defined scalar and subrange types are taken up first, followed by arrays, records, pointers, files, and sets. A chapter on searching and sorting illustrates two important applications of arrays.

The **goto** statement is relegated to an appendix, as befits its lack of importance in Pascal. The appendix briefly illustrates two uses of **goto** statements: jumping out of loops and jumping out of procedures. Students are cautioned to use **goto** statements only in those rare situations where none of the standard Pascal control structures are more suitable.

This text uses the publication form of Pascal—programs are written in lower case letters: boldface for reserved words and italics for identifiers. The different typefaces help students distinguished the different kinds of symbols appearing in programs. The lower case letters encourage students to use ordinary handwriting for their own programs, instead of laboriously printed capital letters. To help students enter their programs into a computer and interpret the printout they receive back, chapter 2 includes a discussion of hardware versions of Pascal.

Pascal syntax is presented through explanations and illustrations instead of syntax diagrams. As useful as the latter are to accomplished programmers, they are apt to be more confusing than helpful to beginners, who have enough trouble learning a programming language without having to learn a metalanguage as well.

The principles of program design, such as stepwise refinement and the use of functions and procedures as modules, are presented mainly by example. Students need much practical experience with these techniques before theoretical discussions of them can be meaningful. Stepwise refinement is used only when the complexity of the program calls for it; it is not used for programs so simple as to render it trivial.

The version of Pascal presented here is Standard Pascal, as defined in Jensen and Wirth, *Pascal User Manual and Report* (Springer-Verlag, 1974). Students are given the customary warnng that particular implementations of Pascal may differ in some respects from the version described in the text.

ACKNOWLEDGMENTS

I am most grateful to Bob Mathis and Sandra Mitchell for their valuable comments on the manuscript.

INTRODUCTION
TO PASCAL

Chapter 1

COMPUTERS, PROGRAMS, AND PROGRAMMING LANGUAGES

Computers are machines used for processing information. The information processing that a computer does is controlled by a detailed set of step-by-step instructions called a *program*. By changing the program we can change completely the kind of information processing a given computer does. A single computer can do such diverse jobs as working out the orbit of a spacecraft, making up a payroll, and playing chess, provided only that it is given the necessary instructions for carrying out each task. Because of this flexibility, the computer is sometimes called an "all-purpose machine."

The art and craft of preparing instructions for computers to follow is known as *programming*, and a person who does this job is a *programmer*. The program is expressed in a *programming language*. When the computer carries out the instructions in a program, it is said to *execute* the program.

In this book you will learn how to write programs in a programming language called *Pascal*. (The language is named in honor of the 17th century French mathematician Blaise Pascal, who designed and built one of the world's first mechanical calculators.) We will begin our study of Pascal in the following chapter. But first, we will find it helpful to orient ourselves by looking briefly at some of the general properties of information, computers, and programming languages.

INFORMATION, DATA, AND BINARY CODES

We can define *information* as the facts and ideas that human beings convey to one another. When these facts and ideas are inside our heads we refer to them as *knowledge*. But when we pass them on to other people or record them in books,

1

they become information. We can think of information as knowledge in the process of being conveyed from one person to another.

Information, like knowledge, is an abstract concept, and we cannot use abstractions to communicate with one another. Instead we have to use concrete, physical symbols, such as the sounds of our voices, the letters of the alphabet, or the electric currents flowing in a telephone line. Physical symbols that represent information are known as *data*.

For example, consider the sentence

ATLANTA IS THE CAPITAL OF GEORGIA

The information that this sentence conveys is the fact that Atlanta is the capital of the state of Georgia. The data that represents this information consists of the letter A followed by the letter T followed by the letter L, and so on.

A computer processes information by manipulating the physical symbols—the data—that represent the information. For this reason we can also say that computers are data processing machines. Data is never processed for its own sake, however, but only for the sake of the information it represents. In the computer industry the terms "information processing" and "data processing" are both widely used to describe what a computer does.

Binary Codes

Computer engineers have found that the most convenient and reliable way to represent information inside a computer is to use devices each of which can be in only one of two possible states. For example, an electric circuit may either have a current flowing in it or have no current flowing in it; at a certain point in the computer there will be either a voltage present or no voltage present; at a particular position on a card there will be either a hole punched or no hole punched.

Programmers use the symbols 0 (zero) and 1 (one) to represent these two possible states. The 1 might represent a current flowing and the 0 might represent no current flowing. Or the 1 could represent a punched hole and the 0 would represent the absence of a punched hole. Fortunately, we do not have to worry about exactly what the 0s and 1s represent—we can leave that to the computer engineers. All we need to know is that information is represented inside computers in ways that correspond to certain combinations of the two symbols 0 and 1.

The symbols 0 and 1 are known as *binary digits*, or *bits* for short. Any scheme for representing information using combinations of 0s and 1s is known as a *binary code*.

For example, in one popular scheme for coding the letters of the alphabet, each letter is represented by seven bits. In this code, the word COMPUTER is represented as follows:

1000011	1001111	1001101	1010000
C	O	M	P

1010101	1010100	1000101	1010010
U	T	E	R

Numbers are usually represented inside computers using *binary notation*—a number system that uses only the digits 0 (zero) and 1 (one) instead of the usual 0–9. The best way to visualize binary notation is to think of a counter, such as the mileage indicator on an automobile. But suppose that each dial has only the two digits 0 and 1 instead of the the ten digits 0–9. When the car left the factory the indicator would read

0000

and after the car had traveled one mile it would read

0001

Now, when the car travels another mile, the rightmost digit will turn back to 0. But in doing so it will cause the digit second from the right to advance one position, the same thing that takes place on an ordinary mileage indicator when a digit goes from 9 back to 0. So after the car has traveled a total of two miles the reading will be

0010

and after the car has traveled three miles the reading will be

0011

When the car travels still another mile, our binary mileage indicator behaves like an ordinary one that reads 0099. So after four miles the reading is

0100

after five miles the reading is

0101

and so on.

By now you should have the picture of how binary notation works. The following table shows the binary numbers for 0 through 15 alongside their decimal counterparts. As with decimal notation, we usually omit leading zeros, so that 0001 is written as 1, 0010 is written as 10, and so on. You should have no trouble extending this table to larger values.

Decimal	Binary	Decimal	Binary
0	0	8	1000
1	1	9	1001
2	10	10	1010
3	11	11	1011
4	100	12	1100
5	101	13	1101
6	110	14	1110
7	111	15	1111

COMPUTER HARDWARE

A computer system is made up of *hardware* and *software*. The hardware is the computing machinery itself. The software consists of the programs that the hardware executes.

As is illustrated in Figure 1–1, the hardware of a computer system consists of four major components: the *central processing unit, main memory, the input and output devices*, and *auxiliary memory*. These components communicate with one another over a group of wires (typically 50 to 100) called a *bus*.

Main Memory

Part of the function of main memory is acting as the computer's scratchpad. It holds the data that the computer is currently working with and the partial results that have been arrived at and will be needed again before the job is finished. The program the computer is executing is also stored in main memory.

Main memory is divided up into a number of *memory locations*, each of which can hold a certain amount of information (that is, a certain number of bits,

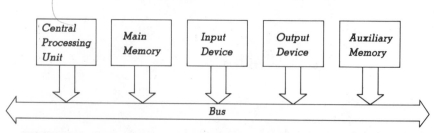

FIGURE 1-1. The hardware of a computer system consists of a *central processing unit, main memory, input and output devices,* and *auxiliary memory.* These components exchange data over a group of wires called a *bus.*

ranging from eight to sixty depending upon the computer). Each memory location has an *address* that is used to designate the location for the purpose of storing information in it or retrieving information from it.

The Central Processing Unit

The central processing unit (CPU) has two functions: (1) it carries out all the actual data manipulations, and (2) it controls the operation of the rest of the computer.

The CPU fetches program instructions from main memory, one after the other, and sees that each instruction is carried out. The CPU itself carries out the data manipulations called for by each instruction. When an instruction calls for the use of main memory or auxiliary memory or an input or output device, the CPU sends control signals over the bus to the designated unit so that it will carry out the required operation.

In the early 1970s it was discovered how to construct a central processing unit on a tiny silicon chip less than a centimeter in length on each side. Such a chip is called a *microprocessor*. Microprocessors can be manufactured in large quantities at low costs. Main memory can also be manufactured on similar chips. Because of the low cost microprocessors and main-memory chips, computers are being used now for such jobs as controlling household appliances, an application that would have once been out of the question.

Input and Output Devices

Input and output devices convert information from the representations convenient for humans to the binary codes the computer requires, and vice versa. There are many different kinds of input and output devices, but the ones programming students are most likely to encounter are *card readers*, *high-speed printers*, and *computer terminals*.

A card reader accepts information that has been punched on computer cards. The cards are prepared using a device called a *keypunch*, which is operated by means of a typewriter-like keyboard. When each key is struck, a particular combination of holes is punched into the card. The card reader senses these punched holes and sends corresponding codes to the computer.

A high-speed printer produces printed output at great speed and in great volume. Some high-speed printers are known as *line printers*, since they print an entire line in a single operation, instead of printing character by character like a typewriter. There are also *page printers* that print an entire page in a single operation. The more advanced printers print tens of thousands of line a minute and use exotic technologies such as laser beams and ink jets.

A computer terminal is a combination input and output device. It consists of a a typewriter-like keyboard coupled with either a typewriter-like printer or a television-like display screen. Information typed on the keyboard is transmitted to the computer. Information returned from the computer is typed out by the printer or (depending on the kind of terminal) displayed on the screen.

Auxiliary Memory

Auxiliary memory is used to store permanent data files and program libraries. Information can be stored in auxiliary memory in larger amounts and at lower cost than is possible in main memory, and the information can be retained for long periods of time. (Information stored in main memory is usually lost when the computer is turned off.)

On the other hand, a much longer time is required to access information stored in auxiliary memory than is required for information stored in main memory. For this reason, information is usually transferred between main and auxiliary memory in large blocks. A block of information is retained in main memory while it is being manipulated. When it is no longer needed for the moment, it is transferred back to auxiliary memory.

Two widely used forms of auxiliary memory are *magnetic tape* and *magnetic disk*.

The magnetic tape used by computers is similar to that used for sound and video recording, and it suffers from one of the same problems. If you have ever tried to locate a particular selection on a tape recording, you know that you spend a lot of time winding and rewinding the tape until you find the part that you want. To locate a particular item on a computer tape also requires time-consuming winding and rewinding. For this reason, computer tapes are usually processed *sequentially*—one starts at the beginning of the tape and processes the items in the same sequence in which they were originally recorded. Thus magnetic tape is called a *sequential access medium*.

A magnetic disk looks something like a phonograph record but it works on the same principle as magnetic tape—information is stored as magnetic patterns rather than in grooves. In use the disk rotates like a phonograph record, and a *read-write head*—analogous to the phonograph needle—is positioned over the part of the disk where information is to be recorded or played back.

The advantage of disk over tape is that just as a phonograph needle can be put down on any part of a record, the read-write head can be quickly positioned over any part of a disk. Thus, regardless of where the information is stored on the disk, it can be accessed quickly without any winding or rewinding. For this reason, a disk is said to be a *direct access* or *random access medium*.

Auxiliary memory is also known as *auxiliary storage*, *mass memory*, *mass storage*, and *secondary storage*.

COMPUTER SOFTWARE

The software of a computer system, you remember, consists of the programs that the computer executes. There are two kinds of software: *applications software* and *system software*.

The applications software consists of the programs that do the various jobs that the computer was purchased to do in the first place. Progams that make up payrolls or play chess or design electronic components or compute the orbits of spacecraft are examples of applications software.

System software, on the other hand, consists of programs that help people write and execute other programs. When the term "software" is used without further qualification it usually means system software, as it does in the title of this section.

Programming Languages

One of the main motivations for system software is to let us program in languages other than the one that the computer hardware can execute directly.

The programming language that the computer hardware is designed to execute is known as *machine language*. Machine language is made up of binary codes for the instructions that are to be carried out and for the memory locations containing the data to be processed. The following short sample of machine language consists of instructions for getting two numbers from memory, adding them, and then storing the sum back in memory:

00100000	Get the first number
00100001	Get the second number
10100010	Add the two numbers
11000100	Store the sum...
00000000	...back into memory

With machine language the programmer has to remember the codes for the various operations the computer can carry out as well as keep track of the locations in main memory where the various data items are stored. Accounting for all these codes is tedious and error prone, as you can well imagine, so programmers avoid using machine language whenever they can.

How can we avoid machine language? Accepting and executing a program written in a particular language is itself an information processing task, one we can program a computer to perform. Therefore, we can write a machine-language program instructing the computer to accept and execute programs written in some other language. We can write programs in any language we wish as long as there is a machine-language program available for our computer that tells it how to process programs written in the language we have chosen.

The first step beyond machine langauge is *assembly language*. Assembly language is quite similar to machine language, except that easy-to-remember abbreviations can be used in place of binary codes for instuctions or memory locations. Thus our sample of machine language might look like this in assembly language:

RCL	TOTAL
RCL	VALUE
ADD	
STO	TOTAL

The abbreviations RCL, ADD, and STO stand for the instructions RECALL (get a value from memory), ADD (add two values), and STORE (store a value in memory). TOTAL and VALUE refer to the memory locations from which data is obtained and in which the result is stored.

Assembly language is a step beyond machine language, but it is not a very big step. In fact it is just machine language thinly disguised. The instructions still call for only very simple operations, such as fetching a value from memory, so that a large number of instructions are necessary to get the computer to carry out any task that is not utterly trivial. And assembly language programs are still dominated by machine-oriented concepts, such as machine instructions and memory locations.

To get around these difficulties, people have devised a number of *higher-level languages*. A higher-level language allows the programmer to tell the computer how to solve a problem in much the same terms that might be used to communicate the solution to another person. The concepts and notation of the higher-level language are those appropriate for the kinds of problems being solved rather than those dictated by the internal workings of the computer.

A large number of higher-level languages have been devised; there are around 170 currently in use. Fortunately for students of programming, the number in *widespread* use is much smaller—around ten. The following are some of the widely used programming languages and their areas of application:

BASIC   Education, personal computing, small business applications
COBOL   Business data processing
FORTRAN   Science, mathematics, and engineering
Pascal   Education and general purpose programming
PL/I   General purpose

The following shows how the addition that we have looked at in machine language and assembly language would be expressed in each of the languages just mentioned:

BASIC   LET T = T+V
COBOL   ADD VALUE TO TOTAL.
FORTRAN   TOTAL = TOTAL+VALUE
Pascal   *total := total+value*
PL/I   TOTAL = TOTAL+VALUE

Language Processors

The programs that make it possible for a computer to execute programs in languages other than machine language are known as *language processors*. There are two types of language processors—*translators* (also called *compilers*) and *interpreters*.

A translator translates a program from a higher-level language into a code that is easier to execute than that of the original program. (When we say a program, such as a translator, does a particular job, we of course mean that the computer does the job under the direction of the program.) In some cases the higher-level-language program is translated into machine language, so that the translated program can be executed directly by the computer hardware. In other cases the higher-level-language program is translated into an intermediate code that must be processed further by an interpreter program.

An interpreter executes a program by fetching and executing the instructions one by one. An interpreter does for a higher-level-language program what the CPU does for a machine-language program. An interpreter can execute a higher-level-language program directly, or it can execute the intermediate code produced by a translator.

Thus a higher-level-language program can be executed using either a translator alone, an interpreter alone, or a combination of a translator and an interpreter. The last alternative is frequently used for the Pascal language.

A program that is not strictly a language processor but that plays an important role in getting higher-level-language programs executed is the computer's *operating system*. This is a supervisory program that oversees the flow of programs and data through the computer. Typically, the operating system accepts a higher-level-language program from the user along with the data the program is to process. It sees that the program is executed using the appropriate language processors. It also sees that the program has access to the data supplied by the user, and that the results produced by the execution of the program are returned to the user.

We can think of the computer hardware, the operating system, and the necessary language processors as forming a *machine* that can accept and execute programs in a particular higher-level language. This machine is named for the language it accepts. Thus we speak of a BASIC machine, a FORTRAN machine, a Pascal machine, and so on.

Since a higher-level-language machine is implemented by programming, a particular computer system can be a BASIC machine one minute, a FORTRAN machine the next, and a Pascal machine the next, depending on which language processor it is executing.

In fact, we can do much better than that. In *time sharing*, a large number of users at computer terminals are connected to the computer at the same time. The computer rapidly switches its attention from user to user. Since the switching is too fast to be perceived by the users, each user seems to have sole use of the computer.

Now the computer may be executing a BASIC language processor for one user, a FORTRAN language processor for another user, and a Pascal language processor for a third. The computer system will seem to be a BASIC machine to the first user, a FORTRAN machine to the second, and a Pascal machine to the third, all at the same time.

For the rest of this book when we refer to "the computer" we will be referring to the Pascal machine rather than merely to the computer hardware.

EXERCISES

1. List as many methods as you can think of for conveying information from one person to another. For each method give the symbols used to represent the information.

2. Show how to represent the numbers from seventeen through thirty-one in binary notation.

3. List some arts, crafts, and professions that make use of special languages or notations.

Chapter 2

PASCAL:
FIRST STEPS

DATA TYPES

A Pascal program can process many different kinds of data, to be used in different ways for different purposes. The different kinds of data are manipulated using different operations, and the data items are represented differently both in Pascal programs and inside the computer. For example, we might want to perform arithmetical operations on numerical data, but expecting to perform arithmetical operations on data made up of letters of the alphabet would not be reasonable.

To help us deal with the diversity of data and avoid silly mistakes like trying to multiply or divide letters of the alphabet, Pascal classifies data into different *data types*. Items belonging to the same data type can be manipulated using the same operations and represented in similar ways both in Pascal programs and inside the computer.

The data items belonging to a particular data type are said to be *values* of that type. For example, one data types consists of integers (whole numbers), so ten, twelve, and fifteen are values of type *integer*.

The particular symbols used to represent values in a Pascal program are known as *constants*. For example, the integer values ten, twelve, and fifteen would be represented as

10   12   15

so that 10, 12, and 15 are *integer constants*.

It is convenient to describe a data type by describing the constants used to represent the values, and this is the approach we will take. But we should not forget that data types are really abstractions independent of the particular symbols used to represent the values.

Pascal has four standard data types: *integer*, *real*, *Boolean*, and *char* (*char* is an abbreviation for "character"). These data types do not have to be defined by the programmer; their definitions are built into the Pascal machine.

The Type *integer*

Integers are whole numbers that do not contain decimal points. The following are examples of integer constants:

25   100   75   1000   523

An integer constant may be preceded by a + or a − sign:

+25   −100   +75   −1000   +523

When the sign is omitted, it is assumed to be positive. Thus +25 and 25 represent the same value.

Commas are *not* allowed in writing integers (or any other kind of numbers) in Pascal. Commas are used in Pascal only to separate items in lists, so using them in constants would confuse the Pascal machine. Thus the following are *not* valid integer constants:

1,000   2,345,975   2,500

There are limits on the permissible values of integers, but these limits vary widely from one Pascal machine to another. On one particular Pascal machine, for instance, integer values must lie in the range

−32767   through   32767   ← PDP

while for another machine the range is

−281474976710655   through   281474976710655   ← VAX   32bit

Your instructor will inform you of any limitations of your Pascal machine that might possibly interfere with your carrying out your assignments.

The Type *real*

For historical reasons, numbers that can have fractional parts (that is, whose constants can contain decimal points) are known as real numbers. The following are examples of *real constants*:

3.5   −2.75   7.943   8.25

A real constant in Pascal is *not* allowed to begin or end with the decimal point. Therefore, the following are *not* valid real constants in Pascal:

235.   .53

Instead we must write

235.0   0.53

As was the case with integer constants, commas may *not* be used in real constants.

Pascal allows another way of expressing real values known as *floating-point notation*. Floating-point notation is convenient when we wish to express very large values (such as 1250000000.0) or very small values (such as 0.000000175) without having to write down large numbers of zeros. You may already be familiar with this notation, since some calculators use a variation of it.

For instance, consider the following example:

1.25E+9

The letter E stands for "exponent" and the number to the right of the E (9 in this example) is called the *exponent*. (In fact, floating-point notation is sometimes called *exponential notation*.) The exponent specifies the number of places that the decimal point should be moved to the left or the right. If the exponent is positive, the decimal point is to be moved to the right. If the exponent is negative, the decimal point is moved to the left.

Therefore to express 1.25E+9 in conventional notation we would start with 1.25 and move the decimal point nine places to the right, adding zeros on the right when necessary. The following shows step by step how we move the decimal point:

1.25	
12.5	one place to the right
125.	two places to the right
1250.	three places to the right
12500.	four places to the right
125000.	five places to the right
1250000.	six places to the right
12500000.	seven places to the right
125000000.	eight places to the right
1250000000.	nine places to the right

Therefore, 1.25E+9 represents the same real number as 1250000000.0. Plus signs in front of exponents can be omitted, so the same value can also be written as 1.25E9.

When the exponent is negative, the decimal point is moved to the left. If we take

1.75E−7

as our example, then we start with 1.75 and move the decimal point seven places to the left. The following shows how we move the decimal point:

1.75
.175   one place to the left
.0175   two places to the left
.00175   three places to the left
.000175   four places to the left
.0000175   five places to the left
.00000175   six places to the left
.000000175   seven places to the left

Therefore, 1.75E−7 represents the same real number as 0.000000175.
    The following are a few more examples of floating-point notation:

Floating-Point Notation	*Conventional Notation*
1.5E3	1500.0
3.1416E2	314.16
2.79E−2	0.0279
475.0E−1	47.5

Floating-point constants always represent real numbers, *even if the decimal point is omitted*. When the decimal point is omitted, it is assumed to occur immediately to the left of the E. Thus in the following the numbers on each line are equivalent:

475E−1	475.0E−1	47.5
1E3	1.0E3	1000.0
1E−4	1.0E−4	0.0001

When the decimal point is used, it must be preceded and followed by at least one digit, just as in conventional notation.
    There are limitations on the range of real values that can be represented inside the computer and on the accuracy with which the values are represented. As was the case with integers, these limitations vary from one Pascal machine to another.
    Notice that although 235 and 235.0, say, represent the same value in ordinary arithmetic, the values they represent belong to different data types in Pascal. The two values are represented differently inside the computer, and some of the operations than can be carried out on them are different. They cannot be used interchangeably in Pascal programs.

Why does Pascal require both real numbers and integers, particularly when some programming languages, such as BASIC, make do with real numbers alone? There are two reasons:

1. All operations on real numbers must keep track of the position of the decimal point, a problem that does not arise with integers. Therefore, arithmetic operations on real numbers are usually more time-comsuming than the corresponding operations on integers.

2. Arithmetic operations on integers always yield exact results. This is not possible for real numbers. For instance, 10.0 divided by 3.0 equals

3.333333333333333...

where the dots stand for an infinite number of additional 3s. Since only a finite number of digits can be stored in the computer's memory, this value cannot be stored accurately. Even if a large number of digits is stored, such as

3.333333333333

the result is still not exact.

The Type *Boolean*

An important feature of computers is their ability to take different actions depending on the conditions that hold true when the program is executed. This makes it possible to program the computer in such a way that it can respond flexibly to its environment.

Therefore, we need to distinguish between conditions that are *true* and conditions that are *false*. For this purpose, we use a data type that has exactly two values, represented by the following constants:

false   *true*

These are often called *truth values* or *logical values* but in Pascal they are called *Boolean values,* in honor of the 19th century English mathematician George Boole, who was the first to develop an algebra of logic.

A Boolean value can be represented inside the computer by a single bit, which is 0 for *false* and 1 for *true*.

The Type *char*

The characters consist of the letters of the alphabet, the numerals 0–9, the usual punctuation marks, and a small number of special signs such as @, $, +, and −. The characters that are available vary from one Pascal machine to another. For instance, both upper and lower case letters may be available on one Pascal machine, whereas another may only have upper case letters.

A *character constant* consists of a character enclosed in single quote marks:

'A'   'a'   '5'   '@'   '$'   '+'   '—'

The quote marks are necessary so that the Pascal machine will know, for instance, that + is a character constant rather than the addition sign, or that 5 is a character constant rather than the integer five.

The character constant whose value is a quote mark itself is represented by *two* single quote marks in succession, enclosed in quotes; that is, by

'''' *quotation marks*

Note that all four quote marks are single quotes—that is, the single quote key is struck four times. The double quote is an entirely different character and has nothing to do with the single quote.

String Constants   A series of characters such as a word or a sentence is known as a *string*. A *string constant* consists of a series of characters enclosed in single quote marks:

'Computer programming is fun'
'ENTER YOUR MOVE, PLEASE'
'23549'
'!#@$%&¢*'

As with character constants, a single quote, or apostrophe, must be represented by two single quotes in succession:

'Don''t go near the water'
'Why aren''t you in school today?'

THE *write* AND *writeln* STATEMENTS

The parts of a Pascal program that specify the operations the computer is to carry out are known as *statements*. The statements are *imperative* statements— each one directs the computer to take one or more actions. (Some other term such as "command" or "instruction" or "order" would probably be better than "statement," but "statement" is traditional.)

A program is of little use if it does not direct the computer to produce output that people can use. For this reason, the statements that cause the computer to produce printed output are among the most important ones in any programming language. In Pascal, these are the *write* and *writeln* statements. *Writeln* is an abbreviation of "write line."

(In this book we will use the terms "printed output" and "printout." On some computer terminals, however, the output will be displayed on a screen instead of being printed. But as far as the program is concerned, there is no distinction between printed output and output displayed on a screen.)

Printing Integers

The *write* statement causes the values to be printed that are listed in parentheses after the word *write*. For instance, the statement

write(1, 2, 3, 4, 5)

causes the computer to print

1   2   3   4   5

When we want the computer to execute several statements one after the other, we write the statements separated by semicolons. Thus

write(1, 2); *write*(3); *write*(4, 5)

causes the computer to execute *write*(1, 2), then *write*(3), and finally *write*(4, 5). Since programs are usually easier to read when different statements are written on different lines, we would usually write these statements as follows:

write(1, 2);
write(3);
write(4, 5)

But notice that even in this form, the semicolons *separate* the statements—there is no semicolon before the first statement and no semicolon following the last one.

When *write* statements are executed in succession they print their values all on the same line, so the statements just given will produce the printout

1   2   3   4   5

the same printout produced by the statement *write*(1, 2, 3, 4, 5).

The *writeln* statement differs from the *write* statement in that *writeln* causes the printer to go to a new line after the specified values have been printed. Thus the statments

writeln(1, 2);
writeln(3);
writeln(4, 5)

cause the computer to print

1   2
3
4   5

Because the third statement of the ones given is *writeln*, the next *write* or *writeln* statement in the program will commence printing on a new line.

The statement

writeln

simply causes the computer to go to a new line without printing anything. The statements

writeln(−10, 5, 9)
writeln;
writeln(−100, 25)

cause the computer to skip a line between the two lines of printed values:

−10   5   9

−100   25

It is usually most convenient to specify printout a line at a time, so we will use *writeln* more often than we will use *write*.

If we are not satisfied with the way the computer spaces out the values on a line, we have the option of specifying the exact spacing that we want. This is done using *field width parameters*.

For example, look at the statement

writeln(−5:10)

The value to be printed is −5 and the field width parameter is 10. The latter specifies that the printed value will occupy a *field* ten characters wide. If the data does not take up ten character positions (as it does not in this case), then the printed value will be preceded by a sufficient number of blanks to make up the difference. If the printed value requires more than ten positions, then the field width parameter will be ignored and the printed value will take up as many positions as needed.

To illustrate how this works, let us underline blank spaces to make them visible. Then the statement just given produces the printout

_ _ _ _ _ _ _ _ −5

The −5 is preceded by eight blank spaces to make up a total of ten character positions. (The underlines, of course, do not appear in the actual printout. The printer simply spaces over eight positions before it starts to print the −5.)

Suppose we print several values, each with a field with the parameter of 8:

writeln(25:8, −100:8, 1:8)

The printout looks like this:

_ _ _ _ _ _25 _ _ _ _ −100 _ _ _ _ _ _ _1

Each printed value is fitted into a field eight character positions wide. In order to accomplish this, 25 is preceded by six blank spaces; −100 is preceded by four blank spaces; and 1 is preceded by seven blank spaces.

When you omit the field width parameters the computer supplies *default values* for them. The default values supplied will differ from one Pascal machine to another, so you must learn what default values your computer uses. If the default values are satisfactory for your purpose, you can omit the field width parameters. Otherwise, you should use them to get the spacing you want.

Printing Real Numbers

When real numbers are printed without using field width parameters, as in

writeln(1.5, −3.25)

most Pascal machines print the values in floating-point notation:

1.500000000000E+00 −3.250000000000E+00

We can use a single field width parameter for each value, just as we did with integers. This still gives us floating-point notation. For example,

writeln(1.5:25, −3.25:25)

gives the printout

_ _ _ _ _ _ _1.500000000000E+00 _ _ _ _ _ _−3.250000000000E+00

To get conventional notation, we use *two* field width parameters; the second parameter specifies how many decimal places will be printed.

writeln(1.5:7:1, −3.25:8:2)

Now the printout is

_ _ _ _1.5_ _ _−3.25

The following is another example of field width parameters for real values:

writeln(3.14:7:3, 9.58:8:4, 1.0:6:3)

The printout is

_ _3.140_ _9.5800_1.000

Printing Boolean Values

Boolean values are printed using the words TRUE and FALSE. For instance,

writeln(true, false)

produces the printout

TRUE   FALSE

Field width parameters can be used to control the spacing.

Boolean values are rarely printed, however. Their primary application is in controlling the execution of the program.

Printing Characters and Strings

The *write* and *writeln* statements handle characters and strings in a uniform way, so we do not have to distinguish between whether we are printing a single character or a string of characters. For instance, the statement

writeln('A', 'b', 'e', 'Abe')

prints

AbeAbe

On most Pascal machines the default is to print no additional spaces with characters and strings. As usual we can use field width parameters to control spacing:

writeln('A':5, 'b':5, 'e':5, 'Abe':5)

This produces the printout

_ _ _ _A _ _ _ _b _ _ _ _e _ _Abe

Notice that

writeln(' ' ' ')

causes the computer to print

'

and

writeln('It' 's a lovely day today.')

gives the printout

It's a lovely day today.

Two quote marks in succession represent a single quote or apostrophe in a string or character constant, and so they are printed as a single quote mark.

A PASCAL PROGRAM

At this point we are ready to write a complete Pascal program:

```
program greeting(output);
{this program prints a message to the user}
begin
    writeln('Good morning.');
    writeln('I am your friendly computer.');
    writeln('Can I do something for you?')
end.
```

When the computer executes this program, it will print

Good morning.
I am your friendly computer.
Can I do something for you?

This program has three distinct parts: a *program heading,* a *comment,* and a *statement part.* Let us examine each one individually.

The Program Heading

The program heading consists of the line:

```
program greeting(output);
```

The word **program** identifies this line as a program heading. Notice that ‹ **program** is printed in boldface. Words printed in boldface are called *reserved words.* The reserved words serve specific purposes in Pascal and may not be used for any purposes other than the ones designated in the definition of the language.

The second item in the program heading is *greeting,* the name of the program. This name was chosen by the programmer. Unlike **program**, *greeting* does not have any preassigned meaning in Pascal. We could just as well have called the program *xyz352.* However, although either name would be acceptable to the computer, to a human being reading the program *greeting* would be by far the better name, since it suggests the purpose of the program and *xyz352* does not.

In Pascal, *identifiers* are used to name things such as programs. Identifiers are constructed subject to the following rules:

1. An identifier must start with a letter of the alphabet.

2. After the first character, the remaining characters of the identifier may be either letters or digits. No other characters (such as spaces or punctuation marks) may be used.

3. An identifier must not be the same as a reserved word. It makes no difference that in the book reserved words are printed in boldface and identifiers are printed in italics, because this distinction is lost when the program is prepared for the computer. Thus *program* is not a legal identifier. A list of reserved words is given in Appendix 1.

4. To save memory, the Pascal machine only keeps track of the first eight characters of an identifier. Identifiers that are intended to be different from one another must differ in their first eight characters. Thus *greeting1* and *greeting2* would be treated as the *same identifier* by the Pascal machine.

The word *output* in parentheses is the name of the file on which the output of the program is to be printed. This file requires some explanation.

In computer programming, any source from which information can be obtained or any destination to which it can be sent is called a *file*. Thus the term refers not only to the permanent data files stored in auxiliary memory but to devices such as card readers, printers, and computer terminals that can send information to the computer and receive information from it.

The files that a program uses must be listed in parentheses in the program heading following the name of the program. For each program two standard files are defined by the Pascal machine: *input* and *output*. Depending on the Pascal machine, *input* could refer to a card reader and *output* to a high-speed printer, or *input* could refer to the keyboard of a computer terminal and *output* to the terminal's printer or display screen.

Since our program *greeting* only outputs information and requires no input file, the file name *output* is sufficient. If it both inputted and outputted information, the program heading would have to be written

program *greeting*(*input, output*);

The program heading ends with a semicolon.

Comments

The line

{*this program prints a message to the user*}

is a *comment*. A comment consists of any text enclosed between the braces { and }. Comments are intended for humans reading the program, not for the computer. The computer ignores any text enclosed between { and }.

Comments may be placed anywhere in the program. Normally a comment is written in one of two ways:

1. The comment is written on a line by itself, as in the example program. This is usually done when the comment applies to the entire program or to a section of a program.

2. A comment can be written on the same line as another statement, as in

> *writeln*   {*skip a line*}

This method is usually used when the comment applies to only one statement, the statement that is on the same line as the comment.

The line following the program heading is a good place for a comment that briefly describes the purpose of the program.

Enough comments should be used in a program so that a person not familiar with the program can understand it. (And "a person not familiar with the program" includes *the programmer* six months after the program was written!) The examples in this book are, for the most part, somewhat undercommented, since the workings of each program are described thoroughly in the surrounding text.

The need for many comments can be eliminated by using meaningful identifiers—that is, by using *greeting* instead of *xyz352*.

The Statement Part

The statement part of the program contains the statements that the computer will execute.

Notice that the statements are bracketed by the reserved words **begin** and **end**. A group of statements bracketed by **begin** and **end** are said to form a *compound statement*. The statement part of a program is always a compound statement.

The statements making up the compound statement are separated by semicolons. Regardless of whether the statements are written on the same line or on different lines, the semicolons occur only between statements. There is no semicolon between **begin** and the first statement and there is no semicolon between the last statement and **end**.

The statements making up a compound statement are usually indented with respect to **begin** and **end**. This makes it easy to see at a glance which statements make up the compound statement, without having to hunt through a complicated program to find the **end** that goes with a particular **begin**. (Although in this simple program there is only one **begin-end** pair, in a complicated program there will be many.)

The period following **end** indicates the end of the program.

Publication and Hardware Versions of Pascal

The example program *greeting* is written in the *publication version* of Pascal—the form in which Pascal programs are written when they are published in books and magazines.

Unfortunately, most computer printers and display devices cannot handle boldface and italics. Some may be lacking special characters such as { and }, and some may not even be able to handle lower case letters.

Consequently, we need hardware versions of the language that use only the characters available on the hardware of a particular Pascal machine. Naturally, hardware versions of the language will vary from one Pascal machine to another. The following illustrates a hardware version of the language where only upper case letters are allowed and where { and } are not available. (When { and } are not available, it is customary to use (* and *) in their stead.)

```
PROGRAM GREETING(OUTPUT);
(*THIS PROGRAM PRINTS A MESSAGE TO THE USER*)
BEGIN
    WRITELN('GOOD MORNING.');
    WRITELN('I AM YOUR FRIENDLY COMPUTER');
    WRITELN('CAN I DO SOMETHING FOR YOU?')
END.
```

The printout is, of course, affected by the restriction to upper case letters, so this program would print

```
GOOD MORNING.
I AM YOUR FRIENDLY COMPUTER.
CAN I DO SOMETHING FOR YOU?
```

Notice that in this (and most other) hardware versions of Pascal, the typographical distinction between reserved words and identifiers is lost. This is the reason that an identifier may never be the same as a reserved word. In the hardware version of the program, it would be impossible to tell them apart.

While we are on hardware versions of Pascal, it is worth pointing out that some details of the Pascal language may vary from one Pascal machine to another. Usually the variations are minor. Your instructor will point out any differences between the version of Pascal described in this book and the version accepted by your Pascal machine.

Another form of Pascal is the handwritten one you will use when working out programs. The usual practice is to use ordinary handwriting for all parts of the program, but to underline the reserved words to make them stand out. Figure 2–1 shows a handwritten version of the example program.

ARITHMETIC IN PASCAL

In Pascal, any combination of symbols that can represent a value is known as an *expression*. Thus the various kinds of constants are examples of expressions:

25   −2.5   *true*   'a'

```
program greeting (output);
{this program prints a message to the user}
begin
    writeln ('Good morning.');
    writeln ('I am your friendly computer.');
    writeln (' Can I do something for you?')
end.
```

FIGURE 2–1. A handwritten version of the program *greeting*. The program is written in normal handwriting, with the reserved words underlined.

Another way to represent a value is to show how that value can be computed. For instance, $3+5$ and $9-7$ represent the values 8 and 2, respectively. These too are expressions.

In an expression such as $3+5$, $+$ is called the *operator* and 3 and 5 are called the *operands*. Since we are interested in arithmetic for the moment, we are interested in *arithmetic expressions*—expressions whose values are integers or real numbers. Consequently, we are interested in the *arithmetic operators*—those operators that operate on integer or real operands and yield integer or real values.

The arithmetic operators for addition and subtraction are, as you might suspect, $+$ and $-$. Unfortunately, we cannot use the familiar signs for multiplication and division, since most computer printers cannot print $\times$ and $\div$. Therefore, an asterisk, *, is used for multiplication. For reasons that we will look at in a moment, three division operators are necessary. They are /, **div**, and **mod**. The following table summarizes the arithmetic operators in Pascal:

+	*addition*
−	*subtraction*
*	*multiplication*
/, **div**, **mod**	*division*

The operators $+$, $-$, *, and / apply to both real numbers and to integers. For $+$, $-$, and *, if both the operands are integers, then the result is an integer. But if either or both of the operands are real numbers, the result is a real number. The following expressions illustrate this for $+$:

Expression	Value
$3+5$	8
$3+5.0$	8.0
$3.0+5$	8.0
$3.0+5.0$	8.0

This scheme is not satisfactory for division, however. The reason is that even when both operands are integers, division may yield a result with a fractional part, as when we divide 3 by 2 and get 1.5. For this reason, the division operator / gives a real result regardless of the types of its operands:

Expression	Value
3/2	1.5
3/2.0	1.5
3.0/2	1.5
3.0/2.0	1.5

There is, however, a way of dividing two integers and obtaining integer results. This is the *quotient-remainder method* that most of us learned in grade school before taking up fractions and decimals. With this method, instead of computing a real number quotient, we compute an integer quotient and an integer remainder:

$$
\begin{array}{r}
3 \quad \text{(quotient)} \\
3\overline{)10} \\
\underline{9} \\
1 \quad \text{(remainder)}
\end{array}
$$

Pascal provides two operators for quotient-remainder division. The operator that computes the quotient is called **div** and the operator that computes the remainder is (for historical reasons) called **mod**. The following illustrates these two operators:

Expression	Value
10 **div** 3	3
10 **mod** 3	1

The *write* and *writeln* statements can be used to print the values of any expressions, and not just the values of constants. For instance, the statements

writeln(3+2, 3−2, 3*2, 3/2);
writeln(3 **div** 2, 3 **mod** 2)

produce a printout similar to the following:

```
5      1      6   1.500000000000E+00
1      1
```

Notice that only the value of 3/2 has been printed as a real number. We can use field width parameters to control the form of the printout, just as we did with constants:

writeln(3+2:5, 3−2:5, 3*2:5, 3/2:5:1, 3 **div** 2:5, 3 **mod** 2:5)

This produces the following printout:

_ _ _ _5_ _ _ _1_ _ _ _6 _ _ 1.5_ _ _ _1_ _ _ _1

EXERCISES

1. Write the following real values in conventional notation:

(a) 3.5E7   (b) 1.25E−5
(c) 150E−2   (d) 1E3
(e) 1E−4

2. Write a Pascal program that will print out your name and address in the three-line format that would be used for addressing an envelope.

3. Write a Pascal program to print out the following price list:

Item No.   Price

297456   4.29
609871   15.95
834789   1.19
984137   25.40

(*Hint*: To make column headings and the columns line up, use the same field width for each column as was used for the column heading.) Make sure you skip a line between the column headings and the columns.

4. Give the data type of the value of each of the following expressions:

(a) 7−4   (b) 6/3
(c) 3.0*9   (d) 25 **div** 9
(e) 17 **mod** 7   (f) 9.0/3.0

5. Write a Pascal program that will work out each of the following arithmetic problems and print the answers. Each answer should be printed on a separate line and identified by means of printed text.

(a)   125+379
(b)   325−150
(c)   65×45
(d)   27÷8   (real-number quotient)
(e)   27÷8   (quotient and remainder)

Chapter 3

USING
MAIN MEMORY

In the previous chapter we saw that by using statements such as

writeln(2543 + 7641)

we could cause the computer to carry out a calculation and print the result. What we did not see was how to save the result of such a calculation so that it could be used again later in the program. Saving results for later use is one function of main memory.

VARIABLES

Named Memory Locations

Main memory, you recall, is divided up into a large number of separate memory locations, each of which can hold a certain amount of data. Each memory location has an address that can be used to refer to it when data is stored in it or retrieved from it. We can visualize main memory as a set of post office boxes, with the box numbers as the addresses used to designate particular locations.

We could refer to memory locations by their addresses, as machine-language programmers do. But it does not take much time spent wondering whether a result was stored in location 1101001011101011 or location 1101001011011011 to drive one mad. Fortunately, higher-level languages such as Pascal offer a better alternative.

In Pascal we can use identifiers as the names of memory locations. We can refer to the locations by their names instead of their addresses. The Pascal machine keeps track of the address corresponding to each name. It is as if we could just put names on our letters and the post office would look up the addresses.

For instance, suppose we have a program that is working with items of merchandise that are taxed at different rates. We might want to keep track of the identification number of the item the program is currently working with and the tax rate for that item. We could use two identifiers, *idnumber* and *taxrate*, to name the memory locations holding the identification number and the tax rate. Suppose the identification number of a certain item is 125439 and the tax rate is 0.035. We can visualize the portion of main memory holding these values as follows:

idnumber | 124539 |

taxrate | 0.035 |

By using the names of these locations in the program, we can order the computer to use the values that are stored in them and to store new values in them.

Because the contents of a location vary as the program is executed and new values are stored in the location, we refer to a named memory location as a *variable*. The name of the location is called the *variable name* and the value stored in the location is called the *value of the variable*.

For example, instead of drawing pictures of memory locations as we just did, we could simply list the values for the variables *idnumber* and *taxrate*:

Variable	*Value*
idnumber	125439
taxrate	0.035

We always refer to variables by their names, just as we refer to our friends Tom, Dick, and Mary by their names. Thus we say that *idnumber* has the value 125439 or that *taxrate* has the value 0.035. Sometimes we abbreviate this even further and say that *idnumber* equals 125439 or that *idnumber* is 125439. All these are shorthand ways of saying that the value of the variable *idnumber* is 125439, and this itself is a shorthand way of saying that the value stored in the memory location named *idnumber* is 125439.

DECLARATIONS

For each variable used in a program, the Pascal machine needs to know the data type of the values that the variable can have.

There are several reasons for this. Values of different data types need memory locations of different sizes; the Pascal machine has to choose a location of the correct size for each variable. Some operators can be applied to values of more than one type. For instance, + can be applied to both integers and reals. The Pascal machine must know the types of values to which the operator is currently being applied in order to carry out the operation properly. Finally, by keeping track of the types of all the values in a program, the Pascal machine can catch silly mistakes such as trying to multiply and divide letters of the alphabet.

Therefore, every Pascal program has a variable declaration part that lists each variable to be used in the program and gives the data type of the values that each variable can have. The four standard data types are represented by the following identifiers:

integer   real   Boolean   char

The variable declaration part of the program comes between the program heading and the statement part.

For example, look at the following variable declaration part:

var
    x: *real*;
    i: *integer*;

The variable declaration part is introduced by the reserved word **var**. Following the reserved word **var** are a number of declarations, each declaration ending with a semicolon. A colon separates each variable name from the following type identifier.

The declarations in the example are

x: *real*;

and

i: *integer*;

According to these declarations, the program of which they are a part uses two variables, *x* and *i*. The variable *x* can have only real values and the variable *i* can have only integer values. We often say, for short, that *x* is a "real variable" and *i* is an "integer variable."

When several variables are declared to be the same type, we can combine their declarations as follows:

var
    x, y, z: *real*;
    i, j, k: *integer*;

These declarations assert that *x, y,* and *z* are real variables and *i, j,* and *k* are integer variables.

As mentioned, the variable declaration part of a program comes after the program heading but before the statement part:

```
program example(output);
{example showing placement of
 variable declaration part}
var
    x: real;
    i: integer
begin
    .
    .
    .
end.
```

The dots between **begin** and **end** stand for the statements of the program.

As is always the case in Pascal, we can arrange the program text into lines in any way that is convenient. In the variable declaration part, it is sometimes convenient to list each variable on a separate line together with a comment describing the role the variable plays in the program:

```
var
    emplno: integer;        {employee number}
    hours,                  {hours worked}
    rate: real;             {hourly pay rate}
```

If we had not wanted to include the comments, we could have written the declaration like this:

```
var
    emplno: integer;
    hours, rate: real;
```

Since the Pascal machine ignores comments and does not care how the program text is arranged in lines, it considers the two sets of declarations to be equivalent.

In the rest of this book we will often be discussing examples that are not part of complete programs. To keep from having to give a declaration part for each example, we will assume that the following declarations apply:

```
var
    x, y, z: real;
    i, j, k: integer;
    p, q: Boolean;
    c: char;
```

That is, without explicitly stating so each time, we will assume that x, y, and z are real variables, i, j, and k are integer variables, and so on.

These declarations are repeated in Appendix 3 for easy reference.

ASSIGNMENT

Assignment is the operation that stores a value in a memory location. Since the value stored in a memory location is the value of the corresponding variable, the assignment operation gives a variable a new value. We say that is *assigns* a new value to the variable, hence the name "assignment."

The *assignment operator* in Pascal is $:=$, and the *assignment statement* has the following form:

variable $:=$ *expression*

When the computer executes an assignment statement, the expression on the right-hand side of the assignment operator is evaluated, and its value is assigned to the variable on the left-hand side of the assignment operator. The assignment operator can be read as "becomes," meaning that the value of the variable becomes the value of the expression.

The simplest kind of expression is a constant. In each of the following, the expression on the right-hand side of the assignment operator is a constant:

$i := 1000;$
$x := 3.5;$
$p := true;$
$c := 'A'$

After the computer has executed these assignment statements, the variables i, x, p, and c have the following values:

Variable	Value
i	1000
x	3.5
p	true
c	'A'

Additional assignment statements can change these values, of course. For instance, if the assignments

$x := 4.8;$
$p := false$

are carried out, then the values of the variables become:

Variable	Value
i	1000
x	4.8
p	false
c	'A'

The only variables that have new values are the ones whose values were explicitly changed by assignment statements. The other variables retain their old values.

Normally, the values assigned to a variable must be of the type that was specified for the variable in the variable declaration part. Only Boolean values can be assigned to Boolean variables and only character values can be assigned to character variables.

There is one exception to this rule. For every integer value there is a corresponding real value. For instance, the real value corresponding to 25 is 25.0; the real value corresponding to 125 is 125.0; and so on. Pascal allows us to assign an integer value to a real variable. When the assignment is executed, the Pascal machine converts the integer value to the corresponding real value. Thus

```
x := 25;
y := 125;
z := 0
```

are permitted. After the assignments have taken place, the values of x, y, and z are

Variable	Value
x	25.0
y	125.0
z	0.0

The reverse is *not* permitted: we cannot assign real values to integer variables. This is because there are no integer values corresponding to real values such as 3.5 and 4.8.

Expressions containing operators can be used in assignment statements, of course. Each expression is evaluated and its value is assigned to the variable on the left-hand side of the assignment operator. The following assignment statements illustrate this:

```
i := 7+5;
j := 9−4;
k := 8*3;
x := 30/8
```

After these assignments have been carried out the values of the variables are

Variable	Value
i	12
j	5
k	24
x	3.75

Variables in Expression

We have said that an expression is any combination of symbols that represents a value. A variable represents a value; namely, the current value of the variable. Therefore variables, like constants, are expressions and can also be used as parts of more complicated expressions.

For example, the following are all valid expressions:

i

j

$i+5$

$10-j$

$i+j$

i/j

When the computer comes to a variable in an expression, it obtains the value of the variable from memory and uses that value in evaluating the expression. For instance, suppose the values of i and j are

Variable	Value
i	9
j	6

Then the values of the expressions listed above are as follows:

Expression	Value
i	9
j	6
$i+5$	14
$10-j$	4
$i+j$	15
i/j	1.5

Expressions containing variables can be used anywhere that expressions are permitted. For instance, they can be used in *write* and *writeln* statements:

writeln$(i+5, 10-j, i+j, i/j)$

This gives us the printout

14   4   15   1.500000000000E+00

Expressions containing variables can also be used in assignment statements. For instance, the statements

$k := i+j;$
$x := i/j$

assign to k and x the values

Variable	Value
k	15
x	1.5

A few kinds of assignment statements should be looked at in more detail, since they sometimes confuse beginners. For instance, consider the statement:

$k := i$

The variable i is part of an expression, so it represents its value. If the value of i is 9, then this assignment is equivalent to

$k := 9$

and k is assigned the value 9. The value of i remains unchanged, of course.

We can think of this kind of assignment statement as specifying a *copying* operation. The value stored in memory location i is copied in memory location k. Figure 3–1 illustrates this kind of assignment.

In the assignment

$k := i+j$

we can think of the values of the variables first being substituted for the variables in the expression:

$k := 9+6$

The arithmetic operation is then carried out

$k := 15$

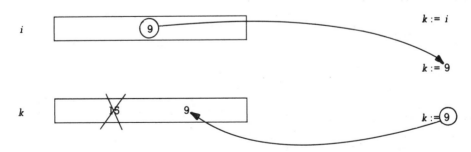

FIGURE 3-1. The assignment $k := i$ can be understood as a *copying* operation: the value in memory location i is copied into memory location k.

and the result is assigned to the variable on the left of the assignment operator. Figure 3–2 illustrates this kind of assignment.

Beginners are sometimes confused by assignment statements such as

$i := i+j$

where the same variable appears on both sides of the assignment statement. But this example is handled just like the preceding one. The values of i and j are obtained from memory and are substituted for the variables:

$i := 9+6$

The result of evaluating the expression is assigned to i:

$i := 15$

Thus the "old value" of i, 6, is used in evaluating the expression. The value of that expression, 15, becomes the new value of i when the assignment takes place. Note that the overall effect of the statement is to increase the value of i by an amount equal to the value of j.

There are two important uses in programming for statements of this kind: *counting* and *accumulating totals*.

Suppose, for instance, we want to count the occurrences of some event, and we want to use the integer variable i as our counter. We start by "clearing" the counter—we set the value of i equal to 0:

$i := 0$

Every time we want to count an event we execute

$i := i+1$

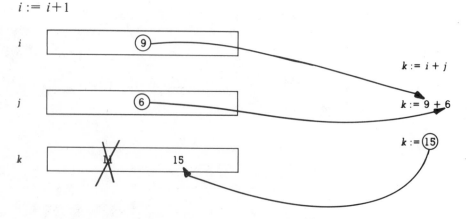

FIGURE 3–2. In the assignment $k := i + j$, the computer first obtains the values of i and j from memory. It then adds those values, and stores the result in k.

which increases the value of i by 1. The following statements and comments show how the value of i changes:

$i := 0;$ {*value of i is* 0}
$i := i+1;$ {*value of i is* 1}
$i := i+1;$ {*value of i is* 2}
$i := i+1$ {*value of i is* 3}
{*and so on*}

Accumulating totals works in much the same way. Suppose we want to use x as the *accumulator*—the memory location in which the accumulating total will be stored. (An accumulator is like the register that holds the running total on an adding machine.) Suppose that the values we wish to add are 3.5, 2.7, 1.9, and 6.3. We start by "clearing" the accumulator

$x := 0.0$

and then proceed to add each value to the accumulator in turn. The following statements and comments illustrate the process:

$x := 0.0;$ {*value of x is* 0.0}
$x := x+3.5;$ {*value of x is* 3.5}
$x := x+2.7;$ {*value of x is* 6.2}
$x := x+1.9;$ {*value of x is* 8.1}
$x := x+6.3$ {*value of x is* 14.4}
{*grand total is* 14.4}

INPUT

Two statements, *read* and *readln*, are used to input values from the standard input file. In most cases the standard input file is either a card reader or the keyboard of a computer terminal.

For example, the statement

$read(i, j, k)$

causes three values to be read and assigned to the variables i, j, and k. Suppose the data was typed at the terminal or punched on a card as follows:

25   6 -100

Then after the *read* statements have been executed the variables have the following values:

Variable	Value
i	25
j	6
k	−100

Successive *read* statements input successive data items, regardless of how the data items are arranged on cards or typed lines. For example, consider the statements

read(*i, j*);
read(*k, x*);
read(*y, z*)

If the data entered is

```
25     40     500
3.5    7.9    2.0
```

then the variables receive the following values

Variable	Value
i	25
j	40
k	500
x	3.5
y	7.9
z	2.0

The *readln* statement reads values for the specified variables and then goes on to the next card or line. Any further data on the current card or line is ignored. For instance, suppose that

readln(*i, j*);
readln(*x, y*)

are executed, and the input data is

```
10     20     4.5   19
6.9    8.5    17    3.5
```

The values assigned to the variables are

Variable	Value
i	10
j	20
x	6.9
y	8.5

Only the values 10 and 20 are used on the first line; the values 4.5 and 19 are skipped over. Only the values 6.9 and 8.5 are used on the second line; the values 17 and 3.5 are skipped over. The next *read* or *readln* statement in the program must commence reading on a new line.

Recall that when a program inputs as well as outputs values, most Pascal machines require that both the identifiers *input* and *output* appear in the program heading:

program *inandout*(*input*, *output*);

AN EXAMPLE PROGRAM

Now let us look at an example program that uses the features of Pascal that we have taken up in this chapter. We will write a program to compute the sales tax on a purchase and the total amount that must be paid after the tax is added to the amount of the purchase.

The data for the program is the amount of the purchase and the sales-tax rate. For instance, if the purchase were $200 and the sales-tax rate were 4%, then the data would be

200.00   4.0

The program prints the amount of the purchase, the sales-tax rate (it usually helps to have the program print out the data that it inputs), the sales tax, and the total amount to be paid. For the data just given, the printout is

Amount of purchase: 200.00
Sales-tax rate: 4.0
Sales tax: 8.00
Total amount to be paid: 208.00

The program begins by inputting the amount of the purchase and the tax rate:

read(*amount*, *taxrate*)

Before the tax rate can be used in calculations, the percentage must be converted to a decimal—4.0 must be converted to 0.04, for instance. This is done, of course, by dividing by 100.0:

dcmlrate := *taxrate*/100.0

We compute the sales tax by multiplying the amount of the purchase by the (decimal) tax rate:

salestax := amount*taxrate

The sales tax has to be added to the amount of the purchase to get the total amount to be paid:

total := amount + salestax

The program finishes up by printing out the data and results. The complete program looks like this:

```
program tax(input, output);
{This program computes the sales tax on a
purchase and the total amount to be paid}
var
    amount,                 {amount of purchase}
    taxrate,                {tax rate as percent}
    dcmlrate,               {tax rate as decimal}
    salestax,               {tax on amount of purchase}
    total: real;            {total amount to be paid}
begin
    read(amount, taxrate);
    dcmlrate := taxrate/100.0;
    salestax := amount*dcmlrate;
    total := amount + salestax;
    writeln('Amount of purchase: ', amount:8:2);
    writeln('Sales tax rate: ', taxrate:4:1);
    writeln('Sales tax: ', salestax:5:2);
    writeln('Total amount to be paid: ', total:8:2)
end.
```

Like most of the other programs in this book, *tax* assumes that all the data it is to process has been made available to the computer before execution of the program begins. Therefore, the program simply reads the data, does the calculations, and prints the results. There is no provision for any interaction between the program and the user while the program is executing. Most Pascal machines are designed to handle programs and data in this way.

Some Pascal machines, however, permit *interactive programs*. An interactive program can engage in a dialog with the user while the program is executing. Interactive programs are essential for some applications, such as game playing and computer-assisted instruction.

An interactive program is organized in a slightly different way than a noninteractive one. Instead of simply assuming that its data is available, an interactive program must request each data item from the user. (The requests are called *prompts*.) The user enters each data item at a computer terminal in response to the program's request. Also, an interactive program need not print its data with its results, since the user will have entered the data only a few moments before the results are printed.

Here is an interactive version of the program *tax*:

```
program tax1(input, output);
{an interactive version of the sales-tax program}
var
    amount,                    {amount of purchase}
    taxrate,                   {tax rate as percent}
    dcmlrate,                  {tax rate as decimal}
    salestax,                  {tax on amount of purchase}
    total: real;               {total amount to be paid}
begin
    write('Amount of purchase? ');
    readln(amount);
    write('Sales-tax rate (in percent)? ');
    readln(taxrate);
    dcmlrate := taxrate/100.0;
    salestax := amount*dcmlrate;
    total := amount+salestax;
    writeln('The sales tax is ', salestax:5:2);
    writeln('The total amount to be paid is ', total:8:2)
end.
```

The dialog between this program and the user would go like this:

```
Amount of purchase? 200.0
Sales-tax rate (in percent)? 4.0
The sales tax is 8.00
The total amount to be paid is 208.00
```

The user typed the values 200.00 and 4.0. The computer typed everything else.

If your Pascal machine is designed for interactive programming, then when you write your own programs you should be guided more by *tax1* than by *tax*.

CONSTANT DEFINITIONS

In the example programs of the last section we had the sales-tax rate read in as data. This would be appropriate for a program that had to deal with sales in many different localities and hence with many different tax rates. But if a program only has to deal with sales in one locality, say sales at a single store, then the sales-tax rate will be the same for all sales. We can make the tax rate a constant instead of having to read it in as data for each purchase.

On the other hand, even in a single locality the lawmakers will eventually get around to changing the sales-tax rate, and then the program will have to be modified. Therefore, we do not want a particular rate such as 3.5 or 4.0 buried in the program where it will be hard to find when the program has to be modified.

To be sure, it would be hard to hide anything in a program as simple as our example, but in any practical application the statements for the sales tax calculations would be part of a much larger data processing program.

Pascal provides a mechanism for solving this problem. It allows us to use an identifier to stand for a constant. To change the value of the constant we just rewrite the program to change the definition of the constant identifier. All constant definitions are grouped together near the beginning of the program where they are easy to find.

A Pascal program can have a *constant definition part* in which any number of identifiers can be defined to represent constant values:

```
const
    dcmlrate = 0.04;
```

Wherever *dcmlrate* appears in the program, the effect will be exactly the same as if 0.04 appeared. Because of the constant definition, *dcmlrate* becomes another way of representing the value 0.04.

Constant definitions come before variable declarations in the program:

```
program tax2(input, output);
{sales-tax program with constant tax rate}
const
    dcmlrate = 0.04;          {tax rate as decimal}
var
    amount,                   {amount of purchase}
    salestax,                 {sales tax on purchase}
    total: real;              {total amount to be paid}
begin
    read(amount);
    salestax := amount*dcmlrate;
    total := amount+salestax;
    writeln('Amount of purchase: ', amount:8:2);
    writeln('Sales tax: ', salestax:5:2);
    writeln('Total amount to be paid: ', total:8:2)
end.
```

Note carefully that in this program *dcmlrate is not a variable* and new values cannot be assigned to it during execution. *Dcmlrate* is just a synonym for 0.04, and a statement such as

```
dcmlrate := 0.35;
```

is just as meaningless as if it had been written

```
0.04 := 0.035
```

Only a variable name, the name of a memory location, can be used on the left-hand side of the assignment operator.

EXERCISES

1. Suppose that i, j, and k have the following values

Variable	Value
i	~~10~~ 30
j	~~20~~ 10 30
k	~~40~~ 30

and the following statements are executed, one after the other:

$i := i+j;$ $10+20 = 30$
$j := i \bmod j;$ $30 \bmod 20 = 10$
$k := k-j;$ $40-10 = 30$
$j := 3*j$ $3 \times 10 = 30$

Give the values of the three variables after each of the above statements has been executed.

2. If i, j, k are integer variables and x is a real variable, which of the following statements are incorrect, and why?

(a) $i := j/k$ (b) $x := i$
(c) $i := x$ (d) $x := j \bmod k$

integers can't have fractions

3. Write a program that will input a length expressed in feet and inches and output the same length expressed in centimeters. There are 12 inches to a foot and 2.54 centimeters to an inch.

4. Salespeople at a certain company get an 8% commission on their sales. Write a program that will input the amount that a person sold and print both the salesperson's commission and the amount that the company receives after the salesperson's commission has been deducted. Use a constant definition for the 8% commission rate.

5. Write a program to input the values of five real numbers and output their sum.

MORE ABOUT EXPRESSIONS

EXPRESSIONS WITH MORE THAN ONE OPERATOR

In the previous chapters we have seen how to do calculations using expressions such as

$$3+5 \qquad 7*i \qquad i-j \qquad k+5$$

where each expression has at most one operator.

By using enough of these simple expressions we can do any calculation, no matter how complex. But restricting ourselves to these kinds of expressions may not be very convenient. For example, suppose we want to add the values of i, j, and k, and assign the result to the integer variable *sum*. We could do this using two statements as follows:

$$sum := i+j;$$
$$sum := sum+k$$

But how much more natural it would be to write

$$sum := i+j+k$$

and get the same result with one statement instead of two.

An expression such as

$$i+j+k$$

can hardly be misinterpreted. It is obvious that the values of the three variables are to be added, and we will get the same result regardless of the order in which the values are added.

But with an expression such as

$i+j*k$

we must be more careful. We will get different results depending on whether the addition or the multiplication is done first. For instance, suppose that the values of i, j, and k are 2, 3, and 4. The following are two ways we might evaluate the expression:

Addition First	*Multiplication First*
$i+j*k$	$i+j*k$
$2+3*4$	$2+3*4$
$5*4$	$2+12$
20	14

Since we are obviously in trouble if we do not know whether an expression will evaluate to 20 or 14, we need some rules for determining the order in which arithmetical operations will be carried out. Fortunately, the necessary rules are not complicated.

Operator Priorities

To determine the order in which arithmetic operations will be carried out in expressions, the arithmetic operators are assigned *priorities*. For the arithmetic operators there are only two priorities—high and low. The high priority operators are applied first, followed by the low priority operators. Operators with the same priority are applied in left-to-right order as they occur in the expression.

The priorities of the arithmetic operators in Pascal are

*, /, **div**, **mod**	*high priority*
+, −	*low priority*

Thus in any arithmetic expression the multiplications and divisions are done before the additions and subtractions. In our previous example the evaluation labeled "multiplication first" is correct and the one labeled "addition first" is wrong.

The following examples illustrate the use of operator priorities:

Example 1:

$5+7*4$	{*multiplication first*}
$5+28$	{*then addition*}
33	

Example 2:

9*8 − 4*3   {*multiplications first*}
72 − 12   {*then subtraction*}
    60

Example 3:

9*5 + 7 **div** 3   {*multiplication and division first*}
45 + 2   {*then addition*}
   47

Example 4:

1.5*1.1 + 4.5/9.0 − 0.1   {*multiplication and division first*}
1.65 + 0.5 − 0.1   {*then addition and subtraction*}
              2.05

Example 5:

3.6/1.2*3.0   {*since the operators have the*
   3.0*3.0   *same priority, carry out the*
      9.0   *operations in left-to-right order*}

Expressions like the one in Example 5 sometimes cause confusion. The reason is that we confuse the expression with the built-up fraction

$$\frac{3.6}{1.2*3.0} \quad = \quad \frac{3.6}{3.6} \quad = \quad 1.0$$

But the expression in Example 5 is *not* a built-up fraction and it is not evaluated like one. Instead, the operators are applied in left-to-right order, since they have the same priority. Therefore the division is done before the multiplication.

Using Parentheses

But suppose we want to write an expression that is equivalent to the built-up fraction, one in which the multiplication will be done before the division. Is there a way to do this? Yes, the expression

3.6/(1.2*3.0)

will do the job. The parentheses override the usual operator priorities and cause the multiplication to be done before the division. We use parentheses when we want an expression to be evaluated in some way other than the one dictated by the operator priorities.

The rule for parentheses is simply this: Any part of an expression enclosed in parentheses must be evaluated before the operators on either side of the parenthesized expression can be applied. In the expression 3*(4+5)*6, for example, the addition must be carried out before either of the multiplications can be done.

The following examples illustrate the use of parentheses:

Example 6:

3.6/(1.2*3.0)	{*parentheses first*}
3.6/3.6	{*then division*}
1.0	

Example 7:

3*(4+5)*6	{*parentheses first*}
3*9*6	{*then multiplications*}
162	

Example 8:

3*(5*3−7)+7	{*multiplication inside parentheses*}
3*(15−9)+7	{*subtraction inside parentheses*}
3*6+7	{*multiplication*}
18+7	{*then addition*}
25	

Sets of parentheses can be nested one inside the other, as in

3*(5+2*(6−2))

We start with the innermost set of parentheses and work outwards:

Example 9:

3*(5+2*(6−2))	{*innermost parentheses first*}
3*(5+2*4)	{*multiplication inside parentheses*}
3*(5+8)	{*addition inside parentheses*}
3*13	{*multiplication*}
39	

An Example Program

Now let us look at an example program that uses an expression with more than one operator. The program inputs the length and width of a field and computes the area of the field and its perimeter. This information might be of interest to a farmer, for instance, since the area of the field would determine how much could be grown in it and the perimeter would determine how much it would cost to build a fence around the field.

Suppose that the values of the length and width of the field have been assigned to the real variables *length* and *width*. To calculate the area we simply multiply the length by the width:

area := length*width

The perimeter of the field is the distance we will cover if we walk all the way around the field. Suppose we walk along the field, then across it, then along it in the opposite direction, and finally across it in the opposite direction. The total distance we will cover is equal to the value of

length+width+length+width

But this can be simplified, because obviously what we have done is to cover twice a distance equal to the value of

length+width

Therefore, we can calculate the perimeter of the field as follows:

perimeter := 2.0*(length+width)

The following program computes and prints both the area and the perimeter:

```
program field(input, output);
{compute the area and perimeter of a field}
var
    length, width, area, perimeter: real;
begin
    read(length, width);
    area := length*width;
    perimeter := 2.0*(length+width);
    writeln('Length: ', length:7:2);
    writeln('Width: ', width:7:2);
    writeln('Area: ', area:7:2);
    writeln('Perimeter: ', perimeter:7:2)
end.
```

BOOLEAN EXPRESSIONS

Beginning with the next chapter, much of our attention will be focused on methods for controlling the execution of a program, for getting the computer to take the appropriate actions under the conditions that exist when the program is executed.

By a "condition" we mean a declarative statement that can be either true or false. For instance, the statement *the value of i is equal to the value of j*

is true if the value of *i* is 5 and the value of *j* is 5. The statement is false if the value of *i* is 4 and the value of *j* is 3. To determine whether the statement is true or false the computer must actually compare the current values of *i* and *j*.

A condition is represented in Pascal by a Boolean expression—an expression that yields a value of either *true* or *false*. As you might suspect, the expression yields the value *true* if the corresponding condition is true and value *false* if the corresponding condition is false.

Relational Operators

Let us return to the condition

the value of i is equal to the value of j

In symbols we can write this as

$i = j$

We want to consider this as an expression that will have the value *true* if the values of *i* and *j* are equal and the value *false* otherwise.

The best way to do this is to think of $=$ as an operator that takes integer operands (in this case) and yields a Boolean result. Thus $=$ is on the same footing with operators such as $+$ and $-$ except that it yields a Boolean result instead of an integer or real one. We refer to $=$ as a *relational operator*, since the value of *i* $= j$ is *true* only when the relationship of equality holds between the values of *i* and *j*.

To illustrate further, the following are the values of some expressions involving the $=$ operator:

Expression	Value
$3 = 5$	*false*
$8 = 8$	*true*
$4 = 5$	*false*
$0 = 0$	*true*

Pascal has seven relational operators, of which we will consider six here. (The seventh is used in connection with a data type that we will not take up until later.) For each operator there is given a Boolean expression constructed with the operator and the corresponding condition. The Boolean expression yields the value *true* if the corresponding condition is true and the value *false* if the corresponding condition is false:

Expression	Condition
$i = j$	the value of i is equal to the value of j
$i < j$	the value of i precedes the value of j
$i > j$	the value of i follows the value of j
$i <= j$	the value of i precedes or is equal to the value of j
$i >= j$	the value of i follows or is equal to the value of j
$i <> j$	the value of i is not equal to the value of j

The relational operators can be applied to all four standard data types: *integer*, *real*, *Boolean*, and *char*. Before we can make use of the definitions just given, however, we must say what the words "precedes" and "follows" mean for values of each type.

For integers and real numbers, "precedes" and "follows" refer to ordinary numerical order. We say that one number *precedes* another if the first number is less than the second, and that one number *follows* another if the first number is greater than the second. For integers and real numbers, we could substitute "is less than" for "precedes" and "is greater than" for "follows" in the conditions corresponding to the relational expressions.

The following expressions illustrate the use of the relational operators with integers and real numbers:

Expression	Value
$3 < 5$	*true*
$7 <> 7$	*false*
$9 > 8$	*true*
$3.5 < 6.8$	*true*
$7.4 > 9.2$	*false*
$4.2 <= 8.3$	*true*

For the Boolean values, the value *false* is taken to precede the value *true*:

Expression	Value
false $<$ *true*	*true*
false $>$ *true*	*false*

For each Pascal machine there is a *collating sequence* that gives the order for the characters. In every case we may expect to find the letters in alphabetical order and the numerals in numerical order. Beyond that, however, the collating sequence may differ from one Pascal machine to another.

For instance, the following is the collating sequence for Pascal machines that use the popular ASCII (American Standard Code for Information Interchange) character set:

!"#$%&'()*+,−./0123456789:;<=>?
@ABCDEFGHIJKLMNOPQRSTUVWXYZ[\]^_
`abcdefghijklmnopqrstuvwxyz[|} ~

The blank space immediately precedes the exclamation point. The following shows the values of some expressions assuming the ASCII character set:

Expression	Value
' ' < 'A'	true
'0' > 'Z'	false
'C' < 'c'	true
'A' < 'Z'	true
'0' > '9'	false

In practice you usually will be dealing with either the letters or the numerals, and so ordinary alphabetical or numerical order can be assumed. But occasions will arise when you have to worry about the relative order of the blank space, the letters, and the numerals. And if your computer allows both upper case and lower case letters, the order of the upper case letters relative to the lower case letters will be important.

The relational operators are given a lower priority than any of the arithmetic operators, so in any expression involving both relational and arithmetic operators, the arithmetic will be carried out before the relational operators are applied. The following is the revised priority scheme:

*, /, **div**, **mod**	*high priority*
+, −	
=, <, >, <=, >=, <>	*low priority*

The following examples illustrate the evaluation of expressions involving both arithmetic and relational operators:

Example 1:

3+5 < 4*2−1	*{multiplication first}*
3+5 < 8−1	*{addition and subtraction next}*
8 < 7	*{relational operator last}*
false	

Example 2:

10 **div** 3 = 2+1	*{division first}*
3 = 2+1	*{addition next}*
3 = 3	*{relational operator last}*
true	

The Boolean Operators

The Boolean operators **not**, **or**, and **and** take Boolean values as operands and yield Boolean values as results.

The operator **not** changes *true* into *false* and *false* into *true*. That is, **not** *p* is *false* if the value of *p* is *true* and *true* if the value of *p* is *false*. We can define the **not** operator by the following table:

Expression	Value
not *true*	*false*
not *false*	*true*

The expression *p* **or** *q* is *true* when the value of *p* is *true or* the value of *q* is *true or* both. We can define the **or** operator using the following table:

Expression	Value
true **or** *true*	*true*
true **or** *false*	*true*
false **or** *true*	*true*
false **or** *false*	*false*

The only situation in which the value of *p* **or** *q* is *false* is when the values of both *p* and *q* are *false*.

The expression *p* **and** *q* has the value *true* only when the values of both *p* and *q* are *true*. The table defining **and** is as follows:

Expression	Value
true **and** *true*	*true*
true **and** *false*	*false*
false **and** *true*	*false*
false **and** *false*	*false*

The only situation in which *p* **and** *q* has the value *true* is when the values of *p* and *q* are both *true*. In every other case the value of *p* **and** *q* is *false*.

Before we can evaluate expressions involving Boolean operators, we have to incorporate these operators into the priority scheme. The priority of **not** is higher than that of any other operator. The priorities of **and** and **or** are the same as the priorities of * and +, respectively. The following table shows the priorities of the arithmetic, Boolean and relational operators:

not	*high priority*
/, *, **div**, **mod**, **and**	
+, −, **or**	
=, <, >, <=, >=, <, >	*low priority*

There is no general agreement on what priorities the Boolean operators should have, and the designers of different programming languages make different choices. The choice made in Pascal is not the one that is most commonly made.

The Boolean operators are most frequently used in expressions like

$(i = j)$ **or** $(i < k+3)$

Such expressions correspond to conditions stated in English using the words *not*, *or*, and *and*. For instance, the expression just given corresponds to the following condition:

the value of i is equal to the value of j or
the value of i is less than the value of k+3

The parentheses in the expression are mandatory. This is because the Boolean operators have a higher priority than the relational operators. If the parentheses were not present, the Pascal machine would attempt to apply **or** before it applied the relational operators. It would attempt to apply **or** to the values of *i* and *j*, which not only does not make sense, but would result in an error since the values of *i* and *j* are not Boolean and hence the Boolean operators cannot be applied to them.

The parentheses assure that the relational operators will be applied before the Boolean operators. The parentheses also contribute to the readability of the expression, so in this respect Pascal may be ahead of some other languages that assign priorities to the Boolean operators in such a way as to allow the parentheses to be omitted.

Now let us look at a Boolean expression that involves all the rules we have discussed in this section. This expression is much more complicated than those usually encountered in practice:

$(11 < 3*2+5)$ **or** $(6*2 = 4*3)$ **and not** $(2+2 = 4)$

We begin by working out the arithmetic expressions inside the parentheses —multiplications first and then additions:

$(11 < 6+5)$ **or** $(12 = 12)$ **and not** $(2+2 = 4)$
$(11 < 11)$ **or** $(12 = 12)$ **and not** $(4 = 4)$

Continuing to work out the parts of the expression that are in parentheses, the relational operators are applied next:

false **or** *true* **and not** *true*

Of the Boolean operators, **not** has the highest priority

false **or** *true* **and** *false*

The Boolean operator with the next highest priority is **and** and after that comes
or:

false **or** *false*
              false

The value of the original Boolean expression, then, is *false*.

STANDARD FUNCTIONS

Often we need to carry out operations for which no operators are defined. For this
purpose we use *functions*, in which the operation is represented by an identifier
instead of a sign. Pascal has a number of standard functions whose definitions,
like those of the operators, are part of the Pascal machine so that we can use them
without having to define them. In a later chapter we will see how we can define
our own functions. But for now we will stay with the predefined standard
functions.

To see how a function works, let us look at a simple example, the Pascal
function *sqr. Sqr* computes the *square* of a number—the result of multiplying
the number by itself.

To use a function we write a *function designator* that consists of the name of
the function followed by the value to be manipulated, the latter enclosed in
parentheses. Thus

sqr(5)

is a function designator indicating that the function *sqr* is to be applied to the
value 5. The value in parentheses is known as the *actual parameter* of the
function.

The function designator is an expression that represents the value that
results from applying the function to the actual parameter. Thus *sqr*(5) represents the value 25 in the same way that $3+5$ represents the value 8 and $3*5$
represents the value 15. The following are some function designators constructed
with *sqr* and their values:

Expression	Value
sqr(1)	1
sqr(2)	4
sqr(3)	9
sqr(4)	16

Function designators may be used as parts of larger expressions. The values of the function designators are worked out before any of the other operators are applied:

Expression	Value
sqr(2)+3	7
2*sqr(3)	18
2*sqr(4)+3	35

The last example is evaluated as follows:

2*sqr(4)+3	{apply function}
2*16+3	{multiplication first}
32+3	{then addition}
35	

The actual parameter of a function can itself be an expression. In that case, the value of the actual parameter must be worked out before the function can be applied:

Expression	Value
sqr(3+5)	64
sqr(2*3−2)	16
2*sqr(4*3−7)+1	51

The last example is worked out as follows:

2*sqr(4*3−7)+1	{evaluate parameter: multiplication}
2*sqr(12−7)+1	{evaluate parameter: subtraction}
2*sqr(5)+1	{apply function}
2*25+1	{multiplication first}
50+1	{then addition}
51	

Pascal has a number of standard functions. We will look at five of the most useful ones here. Some of the others will be taken up in later chapters.

Function	Definition
abs	computes the absolute value of its actual parameter—if the actual parameter is negative the corresponding positive value is returned; if the actual parameter is positive its value is returned unchanged. Thus *abs*(-5) equals 5 and *abs*(5) equals 5.
sqr	computes the square of the actual parameter. Thus *sqr*(6) equals 36 and *sqr*(7) equals 49.
sqrt	computes the square root of its actual parameter—the value that when multiplied by itself is equal to the value of the actual parameter. Thus *sqrt*(9) equals 3.0 and *sqrt*(2.25) equals 1.5.
trunc	converts a real number to an integer by discarding the part to the right of the decimal point. Thus *trunc*(3.25) equals 3 and *trunc*(3.75) equals 3.
round	converts a real number to an integer by rounding the real value to the nearest integer. Thus *round*(3.25) equals 3, *round*(3.5) equals 4, and *round*(3.75) equals 4.

The actual parameters of *abs* and *sqr* can be either integers or real numbers. The result has the same type as the actual parameter. For *sqrt* the actual parameter also can be either an integer or a real number, but the result is always a real number. For *trunc* and *round*, of course, the actual parameter is always a real number and the result is an integer.

We can say some more about the functions *trunc* and *round*. In a previous chapter, we saw that Pascal permits assignments like

$x := 25$

since to every integer such as 25 there is a corresponding real number. Thus 25 is converted to the corresponding real number and the value of x becomes 25.0.

On the other hand, there is no integer corresponding to a real number such as 6.72, so assignments of real numbers to integer variables such as

$i := 6.72$

are forbidden.

But there are two standard ways of converting a real number to an integer. One way, known as *truncation*, consists of simply discarding everything to the right of the decimal point, so that 6.72 becomes 6. The other is *rounding*, which changes the real value to the nearest integer, with a value such as 6.5 being rounded upward to 7. Thus rounding 6.72 would give us 7.

The functions *trunc* and *round* carry out the truncation and rounding operations. Thus the statements

$i := trunc(6.72);$
$j := round(6.72)$

are valid. The value of i becomes 6 and the value of j becomes 7.

To illustrate the use of functions in a program, let us write a program to compute the diagonal of a rectangular field—the distance one would cover in walking in a straight line from one corner of the field to the opposite corner.

In geometry it is shown that the diagonal of a rectangle is equal to the square root of the sum of the square of the length and the square of the width. That is, if the values of *length* and *width* are the length and width of the rectangle, then the diagonal is computed by the expression

sqrt(sqr(length)+sqr(width))

If the values of *length* and *width* are 3.0 and 4.0, respectively, then this expression is evaluated as follows:

sqrt(sqr(length)+sqr(width))
sqrt(sqr(3.0)+sqr(4.0))
sqrt(9.0+16.0)
sqrt(25.0)
5.0

Notice that the actual parameter of *sqrt* itself contains function designators *sqr(length)* and *sqr(width)*. This is allowed, and our usual rule applies: the actual parameter of a function must be evaluated before the function can be applied. Therefore *sqr(length)* and *sqr(width)* must be evaluated first so that their values can be added to get the actual parameter for *sqrt*.

The following program inputs the length and the width of a rectangle and outputs its diagonal:

```
program diag(input, output);
{compute diagonal of rectangle}
var
    length, width, diagonal: real;
begin
    read(length, width);
    diagonal := sqrt(sqr(length)+sqr(width));
    writeln('Length: ', length:7:2);
    writeln('Width: ', width:7:2);
    writeln('Diagonal: ', diagonal:7:2)
end.
```

EXERCISES

1. Evaluate the following expressions:

(a) 3*2+4*5
(c) 7*3−5

(b) 9 **div** 3*3
(d) 5.7−3.0/2.0

2. Evaluate the following expressions:

(a) 3*(4+5)   (b) (7+4)*(5−3)
(c) (9+7) **div** 3   (d) 3*(5+2*(7−4))+5

3. Evaluate the following expressions:

(a) 10 < 5   (b) 'A' > 'A'
(c) 9 <= 9   (d) (3 < 5) **and** (2 = 4)

4. Evaluate the following expressions:

(a) *sqr*(9)   (b) *sqrt*(9+7)
(c) 3*round(6.7)+5   (d) *sqrt*(*sqr*(5)+*sqr*(12))

5. The maximum size of a package that can be sent by first class mail is 100 inches in combined length and girth. That is, the length of the package plus its girth cannot exceed 100 inches. Write a program to input the length, width, and height of a package and print out its combined length and girth. The combined length and girth should be computed from the length, width, and height in a single statement.

6. Modify the program of Exercise 5 so that it will also print TRUE if the package can be sent by first class mail and FALSE if it cannot.

Chapter 5

REPETITION

The programs we have written so far may have seemed trivial to you. After all, who needs to write a computer program to work out the sales tax on a single purchase or to compute the area and perimeter of a single field? Rather than write a program it is easier to do the calculation directly, perhaps using a pocket calculator if the numbers are unwieldy.

On the other hand, if we need to compute the sales tax on thousands of purchases or work out the areas and perimeters of hundreds of fields, then the computer makes more sense. By writing the program once and using it hundreds or thousands of times we can save ourselves much labor.

In short, for a computer program to be useful some of the statements of the program should be executed more than once. This repeated use could come about simply because the entire program is used repeatedly. But in most cases, during a single execution of the entire program some of the statements in the program are executed more than once. The programming technique of having a single statement executed more than once is known as *repetition*.

THE for STATEMENT

Useful as repetition is, it must be carefully controlled; a common type of errone-ous program is one that will not stop of its own accord because it instructs the computer to repeat some statements forever. Pascal provides three statements to control repetition: the **for** statement, the **while** statement, and the **repeat-until** statement.

We can introduce the **for** statement by an example. Consider the following:

for *i* := 1 **to** 5 **do**
    write('*')

When the **for** statement is executed, the *write* statement is executed five times. The computer prints:

*****

The *write* statement is indented to show that it is a part of the **for** statement.

On the first repetition the value of *i* is 1, on the second repetition the value of *i* is 2, and so on. We can see this by having the computer execute

for *i* := 1 **to** 5 **do**
   write(*i*:4)

The computer prints

1   2   3   4   5

By using **downto** in place of **to**, we can have the computer count backward:

for *i* := 5 **downto** 1 **do**
   write(*i*:4)

The computer prints

5   4   3   2   1

The values that specify the limits between which the computer is to count can themselves be expressions:

for *i* := 3+2 **to** 4*3−1 **do**
   write(*i*:4)

The computer prints

5   6   7   8   9   10   11

The **for** statement provides for only a single statement following the word **do**. This is not a limitation, however, since the statement can be a *compound statement*—a number of statements bracketed by **begin** and **end** and functioning as a single statement. For instance,

for *i* := 1 **to** 5 **do**
   begin
      read(*j*);
      write(*j*:4)
   end

causes five integers to be read and printed. If the input data is

7   9   3   8   4   1   4   5   0

then the printout produced is

7   9   3   8   4

The repeated statement is considered to be part of the **for** statement. This means that the semicolons separating the **for** statement from the surrounding statements come before the **for** and after the repeated statement. For example, consider the following:

$x := 3.5$;
for $i := 1$ **to** 5 **do** *write*(i:4);
$y := 7.9$

By writing the repeated statement on the same line as the rest of the **for** statement, we emphasize that *write*(i:4) is a part of the **for** statement. Therefore, we are not surprised that the semicolon separating the **for** statement from the statement $y := 7.9$ occurs after *write*(i:4). Usually we write the repeated statement on a line by itself, but the punctuation remains the same:

$x := 3.5$;
for $i := 1$ **to** 5 **do**
    write(i:4);
$y := 7.9$

The same principle applies when the repeated statement is a compound statement. In this case, the **for** statement consists of everything from the word **for** through the word **end** that terminates the compound statement. The semicolon separating the **for** statement from the following statement comes after the word **end**:

$x := 3.5$;
for $i := 1$ **to** 5 **do**
    begin
        read(j);
        write(j:4)
    end;
$y := 7.9$

To illustrate the use of the **for** statement in a program, let us modify our program *field* to print the areas and perimeters for five fields. We assume that the data is arranged in lines (or on cards), with the length and width of one field being given on each line. Thus the data might be as follows

8.6	7.5
6.9	5.2
9.3	.8.6
17.4	14.3
11.5	1.2

The first field is 8.6 by 7.5, the second is 6.9 by 5.2, and so on.
The following is the program:

```
program fields(input, output);
{compute area and perimeter of five fields}
var
    i: integer;
    length, width, area, perimeter: real;
begin
    writeln('Length':10, 'Width':10, 'Area':10, 'Perimeter':10);
    writeln;
    for i := 1 to 5 do
        begin
            readln(length, width);
            area := length*width;
            perimeter := 2.0*(length+width);
            writeln(length:10:1, width:10:1, area:10:2, perimeter:10:2)
        end
end.
```

If this program is provided with the data previously given, then the printout
is as follows:

Length	Width	Area	Perimeter
8.6	7.5	64.50	32.20
6.9	5.2	35.88	24.20
9.3	8.6	79.98	35.80
17.4	14.3	248.82	63.40
11.5	1.2	13.80	25.40

This program is limited in that it will only process the data for exactly five
fields. But, in practice, the number of fields for which the calculation is to be done
will probably be different each time we run the program. We may want to process
the data for five fields one time, ten fields another, fifty fields another, and so on.
One solution is to let the first data item be the number of fields to be
processed. Thus, if we are to process data for five fields the data will be

```
5
8.6        7.5
6.9        5.2
9.3        8.6
17.4       14.3
11.5       1.2
```

whereas if data for only three fields were to be processed, the data would have the
following form:

```
3
8.6      7.5
6.9      5.2
9.3      8.6
```

We want the program to read the first data item and use its value to determine the number of remaining sets of data that will be processed. We can do this by having the program execute the statement

read(number)

and then use *number* in the **for** statement that controls the remainder of the processing:

```
program field1(input, output);
{compute area and perimeter of an
arbitrary number of fields}
var
    i,
    number: integer;              {number of fields}
    length, width, area, perimeter: real;
begin
    writeln('Length':10, 'Width':10, 'Area':10, 'Perimeter':10);
    writeln;
    readln(number);              {get number of fields}
    for i := 1 to number do
        begin
            readln(length, width);
            area := length*width;
            perimeter := 2.0*(length+width);
            writeln(length:10:1, width:10:1, area:10:2, perimeter:10:2)
        end
end.
```

When processing a number of data items and printing the results out in columns, it is often convenient to compute totals for some of the data or results and print the totals at the feet of the appropriate columns. For instance, in the *fields1* program we might want to know the total area of the fields (so we would know how much could be grown on all of them) and their total perimeter (so we would know how much it would cost to fence all of them). Let us modify our program to compute these totals.

We focus our attention on the area for the moment. We will accumulate the total area in a memory location named *totala*. At the beginning of the program we will clear this location to zero:

totala := 0.0

Each time a new area is calculated we will add it to the running total in *totala*:

totala := *totala* + *area*

When the data for all the fields has been processed, the value of *totala* will be the total area of all the fields. The perimeters will be totaled in the same way using another variable, *totalp*:

```
program fields2(input, output);
{compute area and perimeter of an
arbitrary number of fields together
with total area and total perimeter
of all the fields}
var
    i,
    number: integer;          {number of fields}
    length, width, area, perimeter,
    totala,                   {total area}
    totalp: real;             {total perimeter}
begin
    writeln('Length':10, 'Width':10, 'Area':10, 'Perimeter':10);
    writeln;
    totala := 0.0;            {clear accumulators}
    totalp := 0.0;
    readln(number);           {get number of fields}
    for i := 1 to number do
        begin
            readln(length, width);
            area := length*width;
            perimeter := 2.0*(length+width);
            writeln(length:10:1, width:10:1, area:10:2, perimeter:10:2);
            totala := totala+area;     {accumulate totals}
            totalp := totalp+perimeter
        end
    {print totals}
    writeln;
    writeln(totala:30:2, totalp:10:2)
end.
```

Suppose that the data for this program is

```
3
8.6    7.5
6.9    5.2
9.3    8.6
```

The computer produces the following printout:

Length	Width	Area	Perimeter
8.6	7.5	64.50	32.20
6.9	5.2	35.88	24.20
9.3	8.6	79.98	35.80
		180.36	92.20

THE while STATEMENT

In order to use the **for** statement we need to know the number of repetitions that are to be carried out before any of the repetitions are done. But sometimes we may want to execute a statement repeatedly while a certain condition is true. We do not have to know in advance how many repetitions will take place before the condition becomes false. The **while** statement allows us to control repetition in this way.

The **while** statement has the general form

while *Boolean expression* **do**
  statement

The Boolean expression is evaluated, and if its value is *true*, the statement is executed. This process is repeated as long as the Boolean expression has the value *true* when it is evaluated. When the Boolean expression is evaluated and found to have the value *false*, the repetition terminates and the computer goes on to the next statement in the program. As with the **for** statement, the repeated statement can be either a simple or a compound statement.

For example, consider the following:

```
i := 0;
while i <= 20 do
    i := i+5
```

This causes the statement $i := i+5$ to be executed repeatedly. Since each execution increases the value of i by 5, i takes on the values 0, 5, 10, 15, 20, 25. Before each repetition the value of i is checked to see if it is less than or equal to 20. When the value of i is 0, 5, 10, 15, or 20, this test is passed and the repeated statement is executed. But when the value of i is 25, the value of $i <= 20$ is *false*, so the repetitions are terminated and the computer goes on to the next statement in the program.

We can get the successive values of i printed out by using a compound statement as the repeated statement:

```
i := 0;
while i <= 20 do
    begin
        write(i:4);
        i := i+5
    end
```

These statements cause the computer to print

0   5   10   15   20

Note that the final value of i, 25, is not printed. Why?

Since the **while** statement checks the value of the Boolean expression before each execution of the repeated statement, no executions at all will take place if the Boolean expression is *false* the first time it is checked. For example, consider the statements

```
i := 21;
while i <= 20 do
    begin
        write(i:4);
        i := i+5
    end
```

No values are printed. Since $i <= 20$ is *false* the first time it is evaluated, the repeated statement is not executed, no printing takes place, and the value of i remains 21.

Predicates

Functions that yield Boolean values are, for historical reasons, known as *predicates*. Pascal has three standard predicates, one of which is particularly useful in connection with the **while** statement.

The following are the three predicates:

Predicate	*Definition*
odd	The actual parameter is an integer. The value of odd(i) is *true* if the value of i is an odd number and *false* otherwise. Thus odd(4) equals *false* and odd(5) equals *true*.
eof	The actual parameter is a file such as *input*. The value of eof(f) is *true* if no more data remains to be read from file f ("eof" stands for "end of file").
eoln	The actual parameter is a file such as *input*. The value of eoln(f) is *true* if the end of the current line has been reached ("eoln" stands for "end of line"). When the computer goes to a new line, the value of eoln becomes *false* again.

More detailed definitions of *eof* and *eoln* will be found in Chapter 12. The definitions just given will serve until then. Pascal allows the actual parameter for these functions to be omitted. When the actual parameter is omitted, Pascal assumes it to be *input*. Thus

eof	is equivalent to	*eof(input)*
eoln	is equivalent to	*eoln(input)*

Using *eof*

The most useful of the predicates turns out to be *eof*, and the reason is this: In the previous section we arranged for the program to process an arbitrary number of sets of data by letting the first data item be the number of sets of data to be processed. If the number of sets of data to be processed is large, this approach is not practical. To use it, we would have to count the sets of data, and if there are thousands of them, the labor of counting them would be tremendous.

By using the *eof* predicate we can avoid having to count the sets of data. We simply continue processing while there is still data remaining to be processed—that is, while the value of *eof(input)* is *false* or while the value of **not** *eof(input)* is true.

For example, let us write a simple payroll program. For each employee the program reads the employee's ID number, the hours the employee worked, and the amount per hour that the employee is paid. The program prints this information together with the amount the employee is to be paid:

```
program payroll(input, output);
{compute employees' wages}
var
    idnumber: integer;
    hours,        {hours worked}
    rate,         {amount paid per hour}
    wages: real;
begin
    writeln ('ID Number':10, 'Hours'10, 'Rate':10, 'Wages':10);
    writeln;
    while not eof (input) do
        begin
            readln(idnumber, hours, rate);
            wages := hours*rate;
            writeln(idnumber:10, hours:10:1, rate:10:2, wages:10:2)
        end
end.
```

The *readln* statement rather than the *read* statement should be used in this kind of program. *Readln* causes the computer to attempt to go to a new line after it has read the data on the current one. If there are no more lines, the computer notes this fact and gives *eof(input)* the value *true* on the next time that predicate is evaluated. Since *read* does not attempt to go to a new line after having read the data on one line, the computer will not discover that there are no more lines until it actually attempts to read data from a nonexistent line.

Using Sentinels

Another way to detect the end of the data is to give the last data item a special value. The computer processes data until it comes upon this special value. A data value used in this way is called a *sentinel*. Sentinels are particularly useful when one file contains several sets of data to be processed, so that the end of a set of data does not necessarily coincide with the end of the file.

Let us modify the *payroll* program to use a sentinel. The last data item will consist of an ID number of 999999. This value for the ID number will signal the end of the data:

```pascal
program payroll1(input, output);
{payroll program using a sentinel
 to detect the end of the data}
const
    sentinel = 999999;
var
    idnumber: integer;
    hours, rate, wages: real;
begin
    writeln('ID Number':10, 'Hours':10, 'Rate':10, 'Wages':10);
    writeln;
    read(idnumber);
    while idnumber <> sentinel do
        begin
            readln(hours, rate);
            wages := hours*rate;
            writeln(idnumber:10, hours:10:1, rate:10:2, wages:10:2);
            read(idnumber)
        end
end.
```

Note that the ID number is read ahead of the rest of the data for an employee so as to check whether or not the ID number has the sentinel value before attempting to read and process the remaining data. Therefore, the ID number for the first employee is read by a separate *read* statement. And after the data for one employee has been processed, the ID number for the next employee is read.

THE repeat STATEMENT

Pascal provides another statement for controlling repetition in addition to the **for** and **while** statements. The other statement is the **repeat** statement, which has the following form:

repeat
    statements
until *Boolean expression*

Any number of statements separated by semicolons can be placed between **repeat** and **until**. Since the words **repeat** and **until** form a natural pair of brackets, no **begin** and **end** are needed.

The statements between **repeat** and **until** are executed, after which the Boolean expression is evaluated. If the value of the Boolean expression is *true*, no more repetitions take place, and the computer goes on to the next statement in the program. If the value of the Boolean expressions is *false*, the repeated statements are executed again (after which the Boolean expression is checked again, and so on).

For example, the statements

```
i := 0;
repeat
    write(i:4);
    i := i+5
until i > 20
```

cause the computer to print

```
0    5    10    15    20
```

After the value 20 is printed, the statement

```
i := i+5
```

changes the value of i to 25. Now the value of

```
i > 20
```

is *true* and no more repetitions take place.

The most important distinction of the **repeat** statement is that the value of the Boolean expression is checked *after* the repeated statements have been executed and not before. This means that the repeated statements are always executed at least once. We can make this distinction clear by comparing two similar sets of statements, one using **while** and the other using **repeat**:

```
i := 21;                           i := 21;
while i <= 20 do                   repeat
    begin                              write(i:4);
        write(i:4);                    i := i+5
        i := i+5                   until i > 20
    end
```

The statements on the left will not produce any printout. The statements on the right will cause the computer to print

```
21
```

When the statements on the left have finished executing the value of i is 21; when the statements on the right have finished executing the value of i is 26.

The difference between the two examples is, of course, that in the example on the left the repeated statements are not executed, whereas in the example on the right they are executed once. This is because the **while** statement checks the Boolean expression before each execution of the repeated statements and **repeat** checks it afterward.

The **repeat** statement is useful when it does not make sense to check a condition until after the repeated statements have been executed. Perhaps the repeated statements read the data that is to be checked or perhaps they calculate the values that are to be compared.

For example, computers are often used to monitor quantities and sound an alarm when a quantity being monitored falls outside a certain range. Hospitals use computer in this way to monitor the vital signs of critically ill patients.

Let us write a demonstration monitoring program. Our program will read values repeatedly as long as those values fall within a certain range. When the values fall outside this range the program prints a warning message. This program needs to use the **repeat** statement, since it does not make sense to check the value of the quantity being monitored before that value has been read:

```
program monitor(input, output);
{program reads values and prints warning
 message when a value falls outside a
 predetermined range}
const
    low = 50;
    high = 80;
var
    quantity: integer;
begin
    repeat
        read(quantity)
    until (quantity < low) or (quantity > high);
    writeln('Monitored quantity out of range.')
end.
```

Notice that the semicolon that separates the **repeat** statement from the following *writeln* statement comes after the Boolean expression.

EXERCISES

1. Write a program to compute the sum of all the integers from 1 through 100.

2. Modify the program *fields2* to use the predicate *eof* to determine when all the input data has been processed.

3. Modify the program *fields2* to use a sentinel to determine when all the input data has been processed.

4. A company gives a bonus to the first salesperson to turn in monthly sales of over $5000. Let the data for a program consist of the ID number and monthly sales for each salesperson, the data items being in the order in which the sales reports were turned in. Write a program that will read this data and print the ID number and sales figure for the salesperson who gets the bonus. Be sure that the program prints something meaningful if none of the sales figures are over $5000.

5. The data for a program consists of a number of integers, each integer on a separate line. Write a program that will read the integers and print them out as long as they are in increasing order. For instance, if the input is

5
7
9
8
3

the program will print

5   7   9

and if the data is

10
15
45

the computer will print

10   15   45

Regardless of whether the program terminates because it found a pair of numbers that were out of order or because there was no more data to be processed, the program should print the message

EXECUTION TERMINATED

below the line of numbers that it prints.

Chapter 6

SELECTION

Selection (also known as *alternation*) allows the computer to select the instructions it will execute depending on the conditions that hold when the program is executed. Selection is essential for providing the computer with flexible behavior. If the computer always had to execute exactly the same instructions regardless of its input or the results of its calculations so far, its behavior would be very rigid and machine-like. But, in reality, computers are now frequently being installed inside conventional machines, such as automobiles, to make the machines more flexible and responsive to their users.

ONE-WAY SELECTION

In one-way selection, the computer checks the value of a Boolean expression before executing a certain statement. If the value of the expression is *true* the statement is executed. If the value is *false* the statement is not executed, and the computer goes on to the next statement in the program.

In Pascal, one-way selection is specified using the **if** statement, which has the following form:

if *Boolean expression* **then**
   statement

When the computer comes to the **if** statement, it evaluates the Boolean expression. If the value of the expression is *true* the statement is executed. Otherwise, it is skipped, and the computer goes on to the next statement in the program. The statement can be either a simple or a compound statement.

As an example of one-way selection, consider the following problem. We want to read the ID numbers and monthly sales of the salespeople who work for a company and print the ID numbers and sales of those who sold more than $1000 during the month.

We will read the data for all the salespeople and use an **if** statement to see that the ID number and monthly sales are printed only for those whose monthly sales were in excess of $1000:

```
program merit(input, output);
{print ID number and sales for those people
 whose sales are greater than $1000}
const
    limit = 1000.0;
var
    idnumber: integer;
    sales: real;
begin
    writeln('ID Number':10, 'Sales':10);
    writeln;
    while not eof(input) do
        begin
            readln(idnumber, sales);
            if sales > limit then
                writeln(idnumber:10, sales:10:2)
        end
end.
```

} Compound statement

TWO-WAY SELECTION

In one-way selection a statement is either executed or not executed. With two-way selection we can specify that one statement will be executed if a certain condition is true and another statement will be executed if the condition is false. Two-way selection lets us select one of two possible statements for execution.

Two-way selection uses a slightly different form of the **if** statement:

```
if Boolean expression then
    statement-1
else
    statement-2
```

Again, when the computer comes to the **if** statement it evaluates the Boolean expression. If the value of the expression is *true*, then *statement*-1 is executed. If the value of the expression is *false*, then *statement*-2 is executed. The two statements can be either simple statements or compound statements.

As an example of two-way selection, let us improve the program *payroll* that we wrote in the previous chapter. In that program an employee's wages are calculated by

wages := hours*rate

This, however, ignores the effect of overtime. Any hours in excess of 40 are considered to be overtime, and the usual rule is "time and a half for overtime." That is, the pay rate for overtime hours is the value of 1.5*rate.

Then we can calculate the wages of someone who has worked more than 40 hours as follows:

wages := 40.0*rate + 1.5*rate*(*hours*−40.0)

In this the term

40.0*rate

pays for 40 hours at the regular rate. The term

1.5*rate*(*hours*−40.0)

pays for the hours in excess of 40—the overtime hours—at the overtime rate of 1.5*rate.

We have two statements for calculating wages, then; one for workers who have worked 40 hours or less, and another for workers who have worked more than 40 hours. We must see that the proper statement is executed for each type of worker. The following program uses an **if** statement to do this job:

```
program payroll2(input, output);
{payroll program with provisions for overtime}
var
    idnumber: integer;
    hours, rate, wages: real;
begin
    writeln('ID Number':10, 'Hours':10, 'Rate':10, 'Wages':10);
    writeln;
    while not eof(input) do
        begin
            readln(idnumber, hours, rate);
            if hours > 40.0 then
                wages := 40.0*rate + 1.5*rate*(hours−40.0)
            else
                wages := hours*rate;
            writeln(idnumber:10, hours:10:1, rate:10:2, wages:10:2)
        end
end.
```

The Blackjack Dealer's Algorithm

In the game of blackjack, a player is initially dealt two cards and has the option of taking additional cards on later rounds. The object of the game is for the total value of the hand—the sum of the values of all the cards—to be as high as possible. The total value must not go over 21, however. If it does, the player "busts" and loses.

On each round after the cards have been dealt, a player has the option of "hitting"—taking another card—or "staying"—electing not to take any more cards. A player hits in an attempt to raise the value of his hand. The player stays if he fears an additional card would make the value of his hand exceed 21.

The blackjack dealer plays a hand just as the players do. But the dealer has no options: if the value of the hand is 16 or less the dealer must take another card. If the value of the hand is greater than 16 but not greater than 21, then the dealer must stay. And if the dealer's hand is greater than 21, of course, then the dealer busts.

In short, the actions of the dealer are determined by a set of rules—an algorithm. It is this algorithm we want to program for a computer.

A futher complication arises in connection with the values of the cards. The cards 2 through 10 are counted at their face values (regardless of suit). The face cards (jack, queen, king) are counted as 10. But the ace can be counted as either 1 or 11. It is counted as 11 if this will not put the value of the hand over 21. If counting an ace as 11 would put the value of the hand over 21, then the ace is counted as 1.

The value of a hand is called the *count*. A count that is obtained by counting an ace as 11 is said to be *soft*. In a given hand no more than one ace will ever be counted as 11, since to do so would always put the count over 21. Therefore, a count can only be soft by virtue of one ace being counted as 11.

We want our program to draw cards until the count is greater than 16, in which case the program will stay if the count is not greater than 21. If the count is greater than 21, the program busts. The data for the program consists of the cards that the dealer could draw. Aces are represented by 1s, cards 2 through 10 are represented by their values, and face cards are represented by 10s. The printout tells which cards were drawn and whether the dealer stays or busts.

For example, if the input data is

5   10   4   7   1   5   10   3

the program would print

The dealer draw a 5
The dealer draws a 10
The dealer draws a 4
The dealer stays
The dealer's count is 19

If the input data is

1   7   3   10   5   4   9   8

the printout is

The dealer draws a 1
The dealer draws a 7
The dealer stays
The dealer's count is 18

Note that the ace is counted as 11.
One final example: if the input data is

8   4   10   9   10   3   1   9

the printout is

The dealer draws a 8
The dealer draws a 4
The dealer draws a 10
The dealer busts
The dealer's count is 22

This program is complicated enough that it is worth the trouble to outline the program before we write the final version. We outline a program by using English-language statements to describe some of the actions to be performed. To get the program from the outline we replace the English-language statements by statements in Pascal. We say that we get the program by "refining" the outline; the entire process is known as *stepwise refinement*.

For example, from what has been said, we know that the blackjack dealer's program must read the values of cards and update the count until the count is greater than 16. Then it must check the value of the count to see if the dealer stays or busts. Let *count* be the variable whose value is the current count. These thoughts lead to the following outline for the statement part of the program:

```
repeat
    read value of card, write value of
    card, and update count
until count > 16;
if count <= 21 then
    writeln('The dealer stays')
else
    writeln('The dealer busts');
writeln('The dealer' 's count is ', count:2)
```

Now we must refine this outline by replacing English-language statements by programming-language statements. The only English-language statement is the one between **repeat** and **until**.

We must therefore write Pascal statements to read the value of a card, write the value of the card, and update the value of *count*. The first two tasks are easy. Let *card* be the integer variable that holds the value that is read. Then to read and print the value of a card we use

```
read(card);
writeln ('The dealer draws a ', card:2)
```

The first step in updating the count is

count := *count*+*card*

and this would be all we would have to do if it were not for the fact that an ace can be counted as either 1 or 11.

Let us use a Boolean variable *softcnt* to record whether or not the count is currently soft. If *softcnt* is *true*, than an ace is currently being counted as 11. If *softcnt* is *false*, then no ace is currently being counted as 11. *Softcnt* is set to *false* at the start of the program.

The statement

count := *count*+*card*

counts an ace as 1. If, however, the count is not already soft, we should count the ace as 11. We can do this by adding 10 to the count (the ace has already been counted as 1, remember). We also set *softcnt* to *true* to record that the count is now soft:

```
if (card = 1) and not softcnt then
    begin
        count := count+10;
        softcnt := true
    end
```

We are still not through. An ace can only be counted as 11 if doing so does not take the count over 21. If the count goes over 21, and the count is soft, then we must count the ace as 1 instead of 11. We do this by subtracting 10 from *count* and setting *softcnt* to *false*:

```
if (count > 21) and softcnt then
    begin
        count := count-10;
        softcnt := false
    end
```

Here is the complete program:

```
program dealer(input, output);
{simulate blackjack dealer}
var
    count, card: integer;
    softcnt: Boolean;
begin
    count := 0;
    softcnt := false;
```

```
    repeat
        read(card);
        writeln('The dealer draws a ', card:2);
        count := count+card;
        if (card = 1) and not softcnt then
            begin
                count := count+10;
                softcnt := true
            end;
        if (count > 21) and softcnt then
            begin
                count : = count−10;
                softcnt := false
            end
    until count > 16;
    if count <= 21 then
        writeln('The dealer stays')
    else
        writeln('The dealer busts');
    writeln('The dealer' 's count is '; count:2)
end.
```

MULTIWAY SELECTION

We have looked at one-way selection and two-way selection. But why stop there? Why not go on and select one statement for execution out of an arbitrary number of possible ones?

This is known as *multiway selection* and there are two ways to accomplish it in Pascal. One way uses the same **if** statement that we have already studied. The other way uses the **case** statement, a statement especially designed for multiway selection.

Nested if Statements

In this section we are going to be talking about a number of Boolean expressions and statements. Let us adopt some abbreviations to make our work easier. We will use $b1$, $b2$, $b3$, $b4$, and so on to represent arbitrary Boolean expressions and $s1$, $s2$, $s3$, $s4$, and so on to represent arbitrary statements.

Using these abbreviations, the two forms of the **if** statement can be written as follows:

```
if b1 then            if b1 then
    s1                    s1
                      else
                          s2
```

These two forms are identical except that the one on the right has an "**else** part." The two forms are often combined as follows:

if *b1* **then**
   s1
[**else**
   s2]

where the brackets around the "**else** part" indicate that it is optional.

Since the statements *s1* and *s2* can be any Pascal statements, they can also be **if** statements. When a statement occurs as part of a statement of the same kind, we say that the statements are *nested*. When *s1* or *s2* is itself an **if** statement, we have nested **if** statements.

Let us look at some examples and see how they work. For instance, if we let *s1* be an **if** statement we get the following:

if *b1* **then**
   if *b2* **then**
     s3
   else
     s4
else
   s2

When the computer executes this statement it starts by evaluating the Boolean expression *b1*. If the value is *false*, then the statement *s2* is executed. If the value of *b1* is *true*, however, then the computer executes the indented **if** statement. Therefore, it evaluates the Boolean expression *b2*. If the value of *b2* is *true*, then *s3* is executed. If the value of *b2* is *false*, then *s4* is executed. We can make a table showing which statement is executed depending on the values of b1 and b2:

b1	*b2*	*statement executed*
false	*false*	*s2*
false	*true*	*s2*
true	*false*	*s4*
true	*true*	*s3*

We can let *s2* be another **if** statement instead of *s1*. This gives us the following:

if *b1* **then**
   s1
else
   if *b2* **then**
     s3
   else
     s4

If the value of *b1* is true, then *s1* is executed. If the value of *b1* is *false*, then the value of *b2* determines whether *s3* or *s4* is executed. Again we can use a table to show which statements are executed for which values of the Boolean expressions:

b1	*b2*	*statement executed*
false	*false*	*s4*
false	*true*	*s3*
true	*false*	*s1*
true	*true*	*s1*

So far all **if** statements have had **else** parts. But of course some of them may not have **else** parts, since the **else** part is optional. When we use nested **if** statements, some of which do not have **else** parts, a small additional complication arises.

Consider the following statement, which is shown indented in two ways, only one of which is correct:

```
if b1 then              if b1 then
   if b2 then              if b2 then
      s3                      s3
   else                 else
      s4                   s4
```

The question is, with which **if** does the **else** part go? The left-hand version shows the **else** part matched with the second **if**, and the right-hand version shows it matched with the first **if**. Which is correct?

The computer, of course, pays no attention to indentation. It cannot, for indentation is optional—we could just as well have written the statement

if *b1* **then if** *b2* **then** *s3* **else** *s4*

as far as the computer is concerned. So the computer is going to execute both versions exactly the same way. One version is correct in the sense that it reflects what the computer is going to do and the other is incorrect in that it is misleading and does not reflect the way the computer is going to execute the statements.

The rule that the computer uses is this: An **else** part always goes with the nearest preceding **if** that does not already have an **else** part. Therefore, the indentation on the left is correct and the one on the right is highly misleading.

Using if Statements for Multiway Selection

We have just looked at several ways in which **if** statements can be nested (and there are other possibilities that we have not looked at). For each different nesting scheme the conditions under which each statement will be executed are different. And some of the schemes have tricky features, such as the problem just mentioned of matching **if**s and **else**s.

Matters would be much simplified if we settled on one particular nesting scheme, memorized its properties, and used it for all our needs. This one particular nesting scheme would constitute a multiway selection version of the **if** statement.

A nesting scheme that can be used to meet many of our multiway selection needs is the following:

if *b1* **then**
   s1
else
   if *b2* **then**
      s2
   else
      if *b3* **then**
         s3
      else   .
         s4

Each **if** statement is nested into the **else** part of the preceding one. The construction can be extended to any number of **if**s. That is, *s4* in the example could be still another **if** statement.

Under what conditions will each of the statements be executed? If *b1* evaluates to *true* then *s1* is executed. If *b1* is *false* but *b2* is *true*, then *s2* is executed. If both *b1* and *b2* are *false*, but *b3* is *true*, then *s3* is executed. Finally, if *b1*, *b2*, and *b3* are all *false*, then *s4* is executed.

Let us again use a table to summarize the conditions under which each statement is executed:

b1	*b2*	*b3*	*statement executed*
true	*true*	*true*	*s1*
true	*true*	*false*	*s1*
true	*false*	*true*	*s1*
true	*false*	*false*	*s1*
false	*true*	*true*	*s2*
false	*true*	*false*	*s2*
false	*false*	*true*	*s3*
false	*false*	*false*	*s4*

Looking at the table, we see a very simple rule for determining which statement will be executed. When we examine the three expressions *b1*, *b2*, and *b3* in the order in which they occur in the **if** statement, we see that the first expression that evaluates to *true* determines which statement will be executed. If *b1* is *true*, then *s1* will be executed regardless of the values of *b2* and *b3*. If *b1* is *false* but *b2* is *true*, then *s2* is executed regardless of the value of *b3*. When both *b1* and *b2* are *false* but *b3* is *true*, *s3* is executed. When all the expressions are *false*, *s4* is executed.

We can think of this kind of **if** statement, then, as representing a list of Boolean expressions and another list of statements to be executed, like this:

b1   s1
b2   s2
b3   s3
       s4

The very simple rule for determining which statement is to be executed is this: go down the list of Boolean expressions until you find the first one that is *true*. Execute the corresponding statement. If none of the Boolean expressions are true, then execute the last listed statement, the one that does not correspond to any Boolean expression.

Previously we wrote this **if** statement in such a way as to emphasize the nesting of one **if** statement inside another. We can also write it in such a way as to emphasize the list of Boolean expressions and the corresponding list of statements:

if *b1* **then**
   s1
else if *b2* **then**
   s2
else if *b3* **then**
   s3
else
   s4

It is this easily understood form of the **if** statement that we will use for multiway selection. It can, of course, contain as many "**else if**" parts as we want, so it can handle as many Boolean expressions and corresponding statements as we want. Also, the final **else** part can be omitted. If the **else** part if omitted, then when none of the Boolean conditions are true the computer simply goes on to the next statement in the program.

Let us apply this form of the **if** statement to a practical problem. We want a program to read students scores and assign letter grades according to the following scale:

Score	*Letter Grade*
90–100	A
80–89	B
70–79	C
60–69	D
0–59	F

Also, as the grades are printed, we want to keep track of the number of As, Bs, Cs, Ds, and Fs in the class. Then when all the grades have been printed the program can print a grade distribution giving the number of students who received each grade:

```
program grades(input, output);
{assign letter grades and compute grade distribution}
var
    stdntid, score,
    acount, bcount, ccount, dcount, fcount: integer;
    grade: char; {letter grade}
begin
    acount := 0; bcount := 0; ccount := 0;
    dcount := 0; fcount := 0;
    writeln('Stdnt ID':10, 'Score':10, 'Grade':10);
    writeln;
    while not eof(input) do
        begin
            readln(stdntid, score);
            if score >= 90 then
                begin
                    grade := 'A';
                    acount := acount+1
                end
            else if score >= 80 then
                begin
                    grade := 'B';
                    bcount := bcount+1
                end
            else if score >= 70 then
                begin
                    grade := 'C';
                    ccount := ccount+1
                end
            else if score >= 60 then
                begin
                    grade := 'D';
                    dcount := dcount+1
                end
            else
                begin
                    grade := 'F';
                    fcount := fcount+1
                end;
            writeln (stdntid:10, score:10, grade:10)
        end; {of while statement}
    writeln;
    writeln('Grade Distribution:');
    writeln('A: ':5, acount:3, 'B: ':5, bcount:3,
            'C: ':5, ccount:3, 'D: ':5, dcount:3,
            'F: ':5, fcount:3)
end.
```

The case Statement

Sometimes we can find an expression whose value determines which statements are to be executed. When this is possible, the **case** statement is easier to use than the multiway selection form of the **if** statement, and the computer can execute the **case** statement more efficiently.

We can illustrate the **case** statement with an example:

```
case i of
    1: s1;
    2: s2;
    3: s3;
    4: s4
end
```

The value of i determines which statement will be executed. If the value of i is 1, then $s1$ will be executed; if the value of i is 2, then $s2$ will be executed; and so on. In this example the value of i must be in the range of 1 through 4. If it is outside that range, the Pascal machine will report an error.

It is possible to label a statement with more than one value. For instance,

```
case j−3 of
    1, 2, 3: s1;
    4, 5: s2;
    6, 7, 8: s3
end
```

If the value of $j-3$ is 1, 2, or 3, then $s1$ is executed. If the value of the $j-3$ is 4 or 5, then $s2$ is executed. And if the value of $j-3$ is 6, 7, or 8, then $s3$ will be executed. In this example the value of $j-3$ must lie in the range 1 through 8, or an error occurs.

The expression whose value determines which statement is to be executed is called the *selector*. The value of the selector is not restricted to being an integer. It can be any of the data types we have studied except *real*. Although it could in theory be Boolean, in practice if we wanted to use a Boolean expression to determine which statement to execute, we would be better off using an **if** statement instead of a **case** statement. That leaves *char* as the other data type we have studied so far and for which the **case** statement is practical. For example, we might use the following to convert a letter grade to a numerical score:

```
case grade of
    'A': score := 4;
    'B': score := 3;
    'C': score := 2;
    'D': score := 1;
    'F': score := 0;
end
```

Now let us use the **case** statement to write another version of the *grades* program. To begin with, we need an expression whose value will distinguish between the grades we wish to assign. A good expression to use is

score **div** 10

The following table shows the letter grades, the ranges of the values of *score*, and the values of *score* **div** 10:

Letter Grade	Score	score div 10
A	90–100	9,10
B	80–89	8
C	70–79	7
D	60–69	6
F	0–59	0, 1, 2, 3, 4, 5

Using the information in this table we can easily write a *grades* program using the **case** statement:

```
program grades1(input, output);
{grades program using case statement}
var
    stdntid, score,
    acount, bcount, ccount, dcount, fcount: integer;
begin
    acount := 0; bcount := 0; ccount := 0;
    dcount := 0; fcount := 0;  zcount := 0;
    writeln ('Stdnt ID':10, 'Score':10, 'Grade':10);
    writeln;
    while not eof (input) do
       begin
          readln(stdntid, score);
          case score div 10 of
              0, 1, 2, 3, 4, 5:
                 begin
                    grade := 'F';
                    fcount := fcount+1
                 end;
              6: begin
                    grade := 'D';
                    dcount := dcount+1
                 end;
              7: begin
                    grade := 'C';
                    ccount := ccount+1
                 end;
```

```
        8: begin
              grade := 'B';
              bcount := bcount + 1
           end;
        9, 10:
           begin
              grade := 'A';
              acount := acount + 1
           end
        end; {case}
        writeln(stdntid:10, score:10, grade:10);
     end; {while}
  writeln;
  writeln('Grade Distribution:');
  writeln('A: ':5, acount:3, 'B: ':5, bcount:3,
          'C: ':5, ccount:3, 'D: ':5, dcount:3,
          'F: ':5, fcount:3)
end.
```

For a still better way to write this program, see Chapter 9, Exercise 1.

EXERCISES

1. A salesperson receives a 10% commission on all sales of $500 or less and a 15% commission on sales over $500. (Thus someone who sold $700 worth would get a 10% commission on $500 and a 15% commission on $200.) Write a program that inputs people's idnumbers and sales and outputs their idnumbers, sales, and commissions.

2. Write a program to input the temperatures that were recorded each hour on a particular day and output the high and low temperature for the day. (*Hint*: Let the values of *high* and *low* at any time be the highest and lowest temperatures that have been inputted so far. Start off by setting the values of both *high* and *low* to the first temperature read. If the temperature just read is greater than the value of *high*, it becomes the new value of *high*. If it is less than the value of *low*, it becomes the new value of *low*.)

3. Suppose that in the data for Exercise 2, each temperature is followed by the time at which that temperature was recorded. Modify the program of Exercise 2 so that it prints out not only the high and low temperatures but the times at which the high and the low were recorded.

4. The program *grades2* will not work if a student's score is outside the range 0–100 (why?). Modify the program so that if the score is outside the range 0–100, the computer will print the student's ID number, the score, and the words INVALID SCORE.

5. The salespeople for a certain company work in three territories, numbered 1, 2, and 3. At the end of each month each salesperson turns in the following data— the salesperson's ID number, the territory number, and the amount sold. Thus

113456   2   375.24

means that the salesperson with ID number 113456 sold $375.24 worth in territory 2. Write a program that will process this kind of data as follows: The printout will consist of four columns. The first column will contain the salesperson's ID number. The remaining three columns will correspond to territories 1, 2, and 3. For each salesperson the amount sold will be printed in the proper column depending on whether it was sold in territory 1, 2, or 3. There will be a total at the foot of each column, which will be the total of all the sales in the territory corresponding to that column. (*Hint*: Use field width parameters to cause an amount to be printed in a particular column. A different *writeln* statement will be needed for each column.)

Chapter 7

FUNCTIONS AND PROCEDURES

When a complicated machine such as an automobile is made, the manufacturers do not start out with the most basic raw materials, such as iron ore or the petroleum from which plastic is manufactured. Instead, the car is assembled out of previously manufactured parts, such as tires, batteries, engines, and radiators. These parts were made by people different from the ones doing the assembly, and sometimes even by a different company.

Functions and procedures are building blocks that allow programs to be constructed out of previously made parts. Using such building blocks has three advantages: (1) When we are working on any one building block we can focus our attention on that part of the program alone. Thus we can break our work down into manageable portions. (2) Different people can work on different building blocks at the same time. (3) If the same building block is needed in more than one place in the program, we can write it once and use it many times.

Building blocks for programs are often referred to as *modules*.

FUNCTIONS

We have already seen how to use standard functions such as *sqr, sqrt, trunc,* and *round*, whose definitions are built into the Pascal machine. Now we will see how to define our own functions to do jobs that were not anticipated by the designers of the Pascal machine.

We define a function using a *function declaration*. As an example, let us define a function *frac* that returns the fractional part of a real number—the part to the right of the decimal point. The following are some examples of *frac*:

Expression	Value
frac(3.14)	0.14
frac(245.75)	0.75
frac(5.0)	0.0

The function declaration for *frac* is as follows:

function *frac*(x: *real*): *real*;
{*returns fractional part of actual parameter*}
begin
    frac := x−*trunc*(x)
end

A function declaration has the same structure as a program with two exceptions: (1) The function begins with a *function header* instead of a program header. (2) There is no period after the statement part.
    The function header for *frac* is

function *frac*(x: *real*): *real*;

The reserved word **function** introduces the function header. Then comes the name of the function, *frac*. Following the name of the function, and in parentheses, the *formal parameters* are declared. The formal parameters correspond to the actual parameters that will be supplied when the function is used. The formal parameter declaration

x: *real*

tells us that the function will take one parameter, which must be a real number. The value of the actual parameter will be assigned to x. Finally, the ": *real*" at the end of the function header specifies that this function will return a real value.
    In the statement part of the function declaration, we have only one statement

frac := x−*trunc*(x)

which computes the value to be returned and assigns it to the name of the function. The value that the function is to return is always assigned to the name of the function. No matter how many statements there are in the statement part, at least one of them must assign a value-to-be-returned to the function name.
    Now let us see how a user-defined function works. Suppose that the following statement appears in a program that uses *frac*:

z := *frac*(3.14)

When the Pascal machine encounters the function name *frac* it sets up a private memory area for the function to use. This private memory area has two memory locations, x and *frac*. Next, the value of the actual parameter is assigned to the formal parameter, x:

$x := 3.14$

Now the statements in the statement part are executed

$frac := x - trunc(x)$

and the value 0.14 is stored in the location named *frac*. When the statement part has been executed, the contents of the location named *frac* are used in place of the function designator in the program that called *frac*:

$z := frac$

So we can think of $z := frac(3.14)$ as equivalent to

$x := 3.14;$
$frac := x - trunc(x);$
$z := frac$

In the statement part of a function declaration, when the function name appears on the left-hand side of an assignment operator, it acts just like any other variable. However, when the function name is used in an expression, it has a different meaning, one that we will go into later. Therefore, for the present, in a function declaration the function name may only appear on the left-hand side of an assignment statement.

The ideas we have been discussing also hold when the actual parameter is an expression and the function designator its itself used in an expression. For instance, the statements

$y := 3.14;$
$z := 2.5 + frac(2.0*y + 0.5)$

are equivalent to

$y := 3.14;$
$x := 2.0*y + 0.5;$
$frac := x - trunc(x);$
$z := 2.5 + frac$

In this example the value 6.78 is assigned to x and the value 0.78 is assigned to *frac*. The value assigned to z is 3.28.

In a program, function and procedure declarations come after variable declarations. The following demonstration program shows how the function *frac* could be declared and used in an actual program:

```
program fracdemo(input, output);
var
    v: real;

function frac(x: real): real;
{return fractional part of actual parameter}
begin
    frac := x−trunc(x)
end; {of frac}

begin {main program}
    while not eof(input) do
        begin
            readln(v);
            writeln(v:10:2, frac(v):10:2)
        end
end.
```

Execution begins with the statement part of the main program. The statement part of the function declaration is executed only when the function is referred to in the main program. Function declarations are on much the same footing as constant definitions and variable declarations—they provide the Pascal machine with information it will need to execute the statement part of the main program.

A user-defined function can have more than one formal parameter. For instance, consider a function that computes the volume of a box given its length, width, and height. The function header for this function could be written

```
function vol(length: real; width: real; height: real): real;
```

However, as in any other variable declarations, we are not required to repeat the identifier *real*:

```
function vol(length, width, height: real);
```

Note that the formal-parameter declarations use the same punctuation as any other declarations, except that no semicolon is used before the closing parenthesis.

The complete function declaration is as follows:

```
function vol(length, width, height: real): real;
{compute volume of box}
begin
    vol := length*width*height
end
```

When this function is called, memory locations for *vol, length, width,* and *height* are reserved in the function's private memory area. The values of the actual parameters are assigned to *length, width,* and *height*. The value that the function assigns to *vol* is returned as the value of the function.

For instance, the statement

writeln(*vol*(9.0, 5.0, 3.0):10:2)

is equivalent to

length := 9.0;
width := 5.0;
height := 3.0;
vol := *length**width**height*;
writeln(*vol*:10:2)

The computer prints the value 135.00.

Lest you begin to think that every function can be defined using a single assignment statement, let us look at a slightly more complicated function. The "factorial" of an integer greater than 0 is defined as the product of all integers from 1 through the integer in question. The factorial of 3 is 1*2*3, or 6, for instance. Let us define a function *factorial* whose value is the factorial of its actual parameter:

Expression	Value
factorial(3)	6
factorial(4)	24
factorial(5)	120
factorial(6)	720

We compute the factorial of the value of *n* by setting a variable *f* to 1 and then multiplying it by each of the integers 1 through the value of *n* in turn:

```
function factorial(n: integer): integer;
{compute the factorial of n}
var
    i, f: integer;
begin
    f := 1;
    for i := 1 to n do
        f := f*i;
    factorial := f
end
```

(Note that the identifier *factorial* has more than eight characters. There is nothing wrong with this as long as no other identifier has the same first eight characters as *factorial*.)

Suppose the program that calls *factorial* contains the following statement:

$j := factorial(5)$

When this statement is executed, the Pascal machine sets up a private memory area for *factorial* containing locations named *n, i, f,* and *factorial*. The statement is equivalent to the following:

```
n := 5;
f := 1;
for i := 1 to n do
    f := f*i;
factorial := f;
j := factorial
```

Here is an error that you may be tempted to make. You might think you could eliminate the need for the variable *f* by writing the statement part of the function as follows:

```
factorial := 1;
for i := 1 to n do
    factorial := factorial*i
```

The reason this will not work is that the function name can be used as a variable only when it appears on the left-hand side of the assignment operator. Therefore the statement

```
factorial := factorial*i
```

is incorrect. We have to use the variable *f* for calculating the factorial and then assign the value of *f* to *factorial* when the calculation is complete.

PROCEDURES

A function is limited in that it can only return a single value to the program that calls it. Often we may want a "building block" to return several values. Or we might not want to return any values at all, but take some other action such as printing a message to the user. A *procedure* frees us from the constraint of always having to return exactly one value.

For example, let us write a procedure that calculates the volume of a box, but prints that value out instead of returning it to the calling program:

```
procedure printvol(length, width, height: real);
var
    v: real;
begin
    v := length*width*height;
    writeln('Volume: ', v:10:2)
end
```

The structure of a procedure is the same as that of a function or a program except that a *procedure heading* is used in place of a program heading or a function heading. A procedure heading is quite similar to a function heading, except, of course, that the reserved word **procedure** is used in place of **program** or **function**. Also no data type is given for a value to be returned, since a procedure does not use the procedure name to return a value.

A procedure is called using a *procedure statement*, which consists of the procedure named followed by the list of actual parameters, in parentheses. For instance, the statement

printvol(9.0, 5.0, 3.0)

causes the computer to print

Volume: 135.00

In fact, the procedure statement

printvol(9.0, 5.0, 3.0)

is equivalent to the statements

length := 9.0;
width := 5.0;
height := 3.0;
v := *length**width*height;
writeln('Volume: ', *v*:10:2)

What we have done, in effect, is to define a new command for the computer to carry out, the *printvol* command. All we have to do is issue the command *printvol* and provide the necessary actual parameters in order to have the computer carry out the calculation and print the result. Once the procedure has been written, we can issue this command whenever we need a volume calculated and printed without worrying about the details of how the computer actually carries out the command.

Variable Parameters

Suppose we want to return the results that a procedure calculates to the calling program instead of printing them out. How can we do this? An obvious way is to use the formal parameters. The formal parameters are used to communicate data from the calling program to the procedure. Why not use them to communicate data in the opposite direction as well?

Unfortunately, the types of parameters that we have used so far are not suitable for this purpose. These parameters are taken to be the names of locations in the procedure's private memory area. Assigning values to these parameters changes the procedure's private memory area but has no effect whatever on the calling program. These parameters are known as *value parameters*, since they can only be used to pass values from the calling program to the function or procedure.

To get around this difficulty, Pascal permits another kind of parameter called a *variable parameter*. Only a variable may be used as the actual parameter corresponding to a formal variable parameter. Constants and expressions are not allowed. The actual parameter corresponding to a variable parameter is, in effect, substituted for the formal parameter throughout the procedure. Therefore, if a new value is assigned to a formal variable parameter, that value is assigned to the actual parameter as well.

For example, let us write a procedure that computes both the volume of a box and its combined length and girth, and uses variable parameters to return the results of the calculations to the calling program. The combined length and girth of a box—the length plus the distance around it in the width-height direction—is computed by the following expression:

length $+ 2.0*(width+height)$

The following is the procedure declaration:

procedure *box*(*l*, *w*, *h*: *real*; **var** *v*, *lg*: *real*);
begin
    $v := l*w*h$;
    $lg := l + 2.0*(w+h)$
end

The thing to notice is that the word **var** precedes the declarations of *v* and *lg*. This indicates that *v* and *lg* are variable parameters, and so can be used to return values to the calling program. On the other hand, *l*, *w*, and *h* are still value parameters, since their declarations are not preceded by **var**. They can only be used to pass values from the calling program to the procedure.

To see the difference between the two kinds of parameters, consider the procedure statement

box(9.0, 5.0, 3.0, *volume*, *lengthgirth*)

where *volume* and *lengthgirth* are real variables declared in the calling program.

Since *l*, *w*, and *h* are value parameters, they are assigned the values of the corresponding actual parameters. Therefore, when the function is called, the following are executed:

$l := 9.0$;
$w := 5.0$;
$h := 3.0$

Since *v* and *lg* are variable parameters, the actual parameters are substituted for them through the procedure. Therefore, *volume* is substituted for *v* and *lengthgirth* is substituted for *lg*. When the statement part of the procedure is executed, the following statements are executed:

volume := *l*w*h*;
lengthgirth := *l* + 2.0*(*w*+*h*)

The overall effect of the procedure statement

box(9.0, 5.0, 3.0, *volume*, *lengthgirth*)

is to assign the value 135.0 to *volume* and the value 25.0 to *lengthgirth*.
Let us see how this procedure might be used in a program to calculate the volumes and the combined lengths and girths of boxes:

```
program volumes(input, output);
var
    length, width, height,
    volume, lengthgirth: real;

procedure box(l, w, h: real; var v, lg: real);
begin
    v := l*w*h;
    lg := l + 2.0*(w+h);
end; {of box}


begin {main program}
    writeln('Length':10, 'Width':10, 'Height':10, 'Volume':10, 'LG':10);
    writeln;
    while not eof(input) do
        begin
            readln(length, width, girth);
            box(length, width, girth, volume, lengthgirth);
            writeln(length:10:2, width:10:2, height:10:2, volume:10:2,
                    lengthgirth:10:2)
        end
end.
```

THE SCOPES OF IDENTIFIERS

The definitions, declarations, and statements that follow a program, function, or procedure heading are known as a *block*. Thus a program consists of a program heading followed by a block. A function or procedure definition consists of a function or procedure heading followed by a block. The following shows the function heading and block for the *factorial* function:

function *factorial*(*n*: *integer*): *integer*;
var *i*, *f*: *integer*; **begin** *f* := 1; **for** *i* := 1 **to** *n* **do** *f* := *f* * *i*; *factorial* := *f* **end**

function heading

block

A variable declaration applies only to the block containing the declaration. It is only meaningful to refer to the variable inside this block. Outside the block containing the declaration, the variable is not declared and a reference to it is meaningless.

The part of the program in which it is meaningful to refer to an identifier is called the *scope* of the identifier. The scope of a variable, then, is the block in which the variable is declared. In the function *factorial*, the scope of *i* and *f* is the block containing the declaration

var
     i, *f*: *integer*;

Only in this block are references to *i* and *f* meaningful.

Now let us consider a program that uses the factorial function to print a table of numbers and their factorials:

```
program printfac(output);
var
    m: integer;

function factorial(n: integer): real;
var
    i, f: integer;
begin
    f := 1;
    for i := 1 to n do
        f := f*i;
    factorial := f
end; {of factorial}

begin {main program}
    writeln('Number':10, 'Factorial':10);
    writeln;
    for m := 1 to 7 do
        writeln(m:10, factorial(m):10)
end.
```

There are two blocks in this program. One block begins immediately after the program heading and extends all the way to the end of the program. The other block begins immediately after the function heading for the factorial function and extends to the end of the statement part of the factorial function.

It is convenient to name a block using the program, function, or procedure name that appears in the program, function, or procedure heading that immediately precedes the block. Therefore, we will refer to the block that begins immediately after the program heading as *printfac* and the block that begins immediately after the function heading as *factorial*.

There is one variable, *m*, whose declaration appears in the block *printfac*. Therefore, *m* may be referred to from anywhere within this block. Since the function declaration is a part of this block, the variable *m* may be referred to from within the function declaration as well. That is, *m* is accessible from both the blocks *printfac* and *factorial*.

The variables *i* and *f* are declared in the block *factorial* and can be accessed from anywhere inside that block. However, *i* and *f* cannot be accessed from any part of the program that is outside the block *factorial*. In particular, they cannot be accessed from the statement part of the main program.

Writing complete programs to illustrate these points get to be rather clumsy. It is convenient instead to use diagrams that illustrate the blocks and the variables declared in them without requiring that we fill in all the details of a program. For the program *printfac* the diagram looks like this:

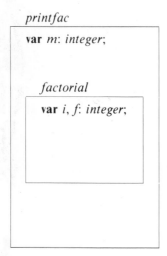

The diagram should make clear the scopes of the variables; *m* can be accessed from anywhere inside the outer block or the inner block; *i* and *f* can only be accessed from inside the inner block. It is helpful to think of the boxes representing the blocks as made of one-way glass. From inside the *factorial* block it is possible to look out and see the variable *m*. But from outside the factorial block it is not possible to look in and see the variables *i* and *f*.

Now let us look at a somewhat more complicated example:

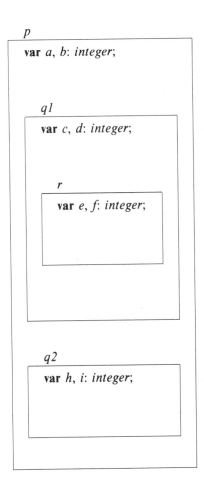

In this example the main program is named *p*. In *p* two functions or procedures (it does not matter which) named *q1* and q2 are declared. Finally, inside *q1* another function or procedure *r* is declared. (Since the body of a function or procedure is a block, that block can, of course, contain other function and procedure declarations.)

The variables *a* and *b* are declared in the outermost block, the main program *p*. They can therefore be accessed from everywhere inside that block. Specifically, *a* and *b* can be accessed from *p*, *q1*, *q2*, and *r*. Variables declared in the outermost block are said to be *global*, since they can be accessed from all the blocks in the program.

The variables *c* and *d* can be accessed from *q1* and from *r*. They cannot be accessed from *p* or *q2*. The variables *e* and *f* can only be accessed from *r*. The variables *h* and *i* can only be accessed from *q2*.

Again, if you think of the boxes in the diagram as made of one-way glass that allows you to look out but not in, you should have no difficulty determining which declarations can be "seen" from any part of the program.

There is one more wrinkle to the accessibility of variables that we have to look at. The following diagram illustrates the problem:

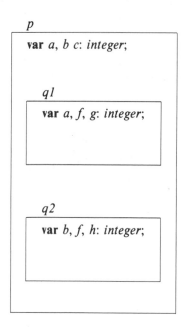

What is different about this example is that the same identifier has been declared in more than one block. Thus there is an *a* in *p* and an *a* in *q1*, a *b* in *p* and a *b* in *q2*, an *f* in *q1* and an *f* in *q2*. This is a permissible practice in Pascal, which is not to say that it is a desirable one.

The first thing to note is that the variables declared in different blocks have nothing to do with one another, even though they happen to have the same names. Thus the *a* declared in *p* refers to a different memory location than the *a* declared in *q1*; the *b* declared in *p* names a different memory location than the *b* declared in *q2*; and the *f* declared in *q1* names a different memory location than the *f* declared in *q2*.

Because of this, a statement can have different meanings depending on where it occurs in the program. For example, if the statement

$$f := 25$$

occurs in the statement part of *q1*, then it will assign 25 to the variable *f* declared in *q1*. If the same statement occurs in the statement part of *q2*, it will assign 25 to the variable *f* declared in *q2*. Since these are two distinct variables, the statement has a different effect depending on where it is located in the program.

Now consider the statement

$$a := 100$$

If this statement is located in *p* or in *q2*, it assigns 100 to the variable *a* declared in *p*.

But what if the statement is located in *q1*? From what we have said so far, there are two variables named *a* that are accessible from inside *q1*: the *a* declared in *p* and the *a* declared in *q1*. We need some rule to tell us to which *a* a statement such as $a := 100$ refers.

The rule is this: When the declarations for more than one variable with the same name are valid at a particular point in the program, then a use of the name refers to the variable having the smallest scope. Thus in *q1* the statement

$$a := 100$$

assigns 100 to the *a* declared in *q1*, since this variable has a smaller scope than the *a* declared in *p*. A little thought will show that this is the only reasonable rule; any other would make it impossible to refer to the *a* declared in *q1* at all.

In the same way, the statement

$$b := b+1$$

refers to the *b* declared in *p* if the statement is located in *p* or *q1*. If the statement is located in *q2*, however, then it refers to the *b* declared in *q2*.

The scope rules for other kinds of identifiers are the same as those for variables. What still needs to be stated, however, is how to determine the block in which a function or procedure name or a formal parameter is declared.

The name of a function or procedure is considered to be declared in the block containing the function or procedure definition. The formal parameters, on the other hand, are considered to be declared in the block that follows the function or procedure heading.

For instance, consider the function outlined as follows:

function *f*(*i*, *j*, *k*: *integer*): *integer*;
var
    m, *n*, *p*: *integer*;
begin

    .

    .

    .

end

We can diagram the scopes of the identifiers introduced in this definition as follows:

f   (*i*, *j*, *k*: *integer*): *integer*
    var *m*, *n*, *p*: *integer*;

The formal parameters, then, are considered to be declared inside the block that follows the function or procedure heading. But the name of the function or procedure is left outside this block, so that it is declared in the block that contains the function or procedure definition. This is necessary so that the function or procedure can be called from the statement part of the block in which it is declared.

We have seen in this section that it is possible to give distinct variables, constants, functions, and so on, the same name, provided they are declared in different blocks. But this does not mean that you should go out and start writing programs in which many different entities all have the same name. Identifiers are not in short supply, and using different ones to refer to different things will contribute immeasurably to the readability of your program. The use of the same name for different things occurs mainly when different people write different procedures and functions. In this case the different people may happen to use the same name for different variables in different functions or procedures. The Pascal scope rules keep different uses of the same name from interfering with each other.

USING GLOBAL VARIABLES

Now let us focus our attention on the most common situation where we have a program with some procedures and functions declared in it. The procedures and functions do not themselves contain further procedure and function declarations. We refer to the variables declared in the program as *global*. The variables declared in each procedure or function are said to be *local* to that procedure or function.

The statements in a procedure or function can refer to a global variable provided there is no local variable having the same name. They can use the values of the global variables and assign new values to them. This provides another way in which data can be passed to and from a procedure or function. The values that are to be passed to a procedure or function can be assigned to global variables before the procedure or function is called. The procedure or function can assign values to global variables and these can be accessed by the main program after the procedure or function returns.

There is a disadvantage in passing data in this way, however. When data is passed using parameters, we can look at the function designator or procedure statement and see at a glance the values that are being passed to a function or procedure and the variables in the main program to which it is being given access. But when global variables are used to pass data, we have to examine every statement in the statement part of the function or procedure to see if it refers to a global variable before we can be sure what data the function or procedure uses and what values it returns.

Because of this disadvantage, the use of formal parameters is usually preferred to the use of global variables. But there are two situations in which global variables are often used:

1. We wish to preserve some values from one call of the function or procedure to the next. This cannot be done using local variables. Every time a function or procedure is called, a new private memory area is set up for the local variables. Any values assigned to these variables are lost when the function or procedure returns. The next time it is called the private memory area will be set up anew.

2. Sometimes, many of the functions and procedures in a program manipulate some common data structure, say a large table. In this case, the table can be assigned to a global variable, and all the functions and procedures can refer to that global variable to carry out their manipulations. We will see examples of this situation later in the book.

A good example of the first situation is what is known as a *pseudorandom number generator*. Pseudorandom numbers are numbers that appear to have been chosen at random but which were actually computed by a function or procedure. Pseudorandom numbers provide the unpredictability in game-playing programs. They also are used extensively in computer simulation where chance occurrences have to be simulated.

Typically, a psuedorandom number generator works with a value called the *seed*, which is the current value of the pseudorandom number. The function or procedure carries out a calculation on the seed to get a new seed—a new pseudorandom number. Each new pseudorandom number is obtained by carrying out a calculation on the previous one.

Let us use a global variable *seed* to hold the current value of the pseudorandom number. The value of *seed* has to be preserved from one call on the pseudorandom number function to the next, since the new value of *seed* is always calculated using the previous value as data.

There are many schemes for actually calculating pseudorandom numbers. The method we will use here is a quick-and-dirty one. That is, it gives a series of apparently unpredictable numbers, but it probably would not be satisfactory for demanding applications where the pseudorandom numbers have to have specific statistical properties. The new value of the seed is calculated in terms of the previous one using the following statements:

$seed := sqr(seed + 3.141592654);$
$seed := seed - trunc(seed)$

That is, a constant is added to the value of *seed* (the mathematical constant *pi* was chosen here) and the sum is squared. The integer part of this result is dropped and only the fractional part is retained. It is largely the effect of dropping the integer part of the result and retaining only the fractional part that makes the resulting series of numbers appear to be random.

Since our calculation retains only the fractional part of the result, our random numbers will be fractions—that is, their values will be greater than or equal to 0.0 and less than 1.0.

Now let us write a function that takes no actual parameters and yields a random fractional value each time it is called:

```
function random: real;
begin
    seed := sqr(seed+3.141592654);
    seed := seed−trunc(seed);
    random := seed
end
```

The variable *seed* is declared in the main program, and a starting value must be assigned to it before the function *random* is called the first time.

We can use the function *random* to generate pseudorandom integers and real numbers in any range that we wish. For instance, suppose that we want to play a guessing game where the computer "thinks" of a number and the player tries to guess the number. (Many computer games are more or less disguised versions of this.) We need to generate random integers in the range of 1–100 for the numbers the computer is to "think of." The following expression will generate a pseudorandom number in the range 1–100:

trunc(100.0*random)+1

We can see that the value of this expression is an integer in the range 1–100 as follows:

Expression	Range
random	0.0–0.9999999
100.0*random	0.0–99.99999
trunc(100.0*random)	0–99
trunc(100.0*random)+1	1–100

The following is the guessing-game program. Notice that it is an interactive program, as all game-playing programs must be.

```
program game(input, output)
{play a guessing game with the user}
var
    seed: real;
    answer: char;
    number, guess: integer;

function random: real;
begin
    seed := sqr(seed+3.141592654);
    seed := seed−trunc(seed)
end; {of random}
```

```
begin {main program}
    writeln('Enter a number between 0 and 1');
    readln(seed); {get starting value}
    repeat
        {play one game}
        number := trunc(100.0* random)+1; {think of a number}
        writeln('I am thinking of a number from 1 to 100') ;
        writeln('You are to try to guess the number');
        writeln('I will tell you whether you are');
        writeln('low or high');
        write('Your guess: ');
        readln(guess);
        while guess <> number do
            begin
                if guess >number then
                    write('Too large. Try again: ')
                else
                    write('Too small. Try again: ');
                readln(guess)
            end;
        writeln('You are correct. Congratulations');
        writeln('Would you like to play again?');
        write('Answer Y (yes) or N (no): ');
        readln(answer)
    until answer <> 'Y';
    writeln('Let' 's play again sometime soon')
end.
```

RECURSION

A function or procedure can call other functions or procedures. For instance, our function *random* called the standard function *trunc*, and the following function calls two other standard functions:

```
function diagonal(length, width: real): real;
begin
    diagonal := sqrt(sqr(length)+sqr(width))
end
```

A function or procedure can even call *itself*. This situation is known as *recursion* and it can be best introduced with an example.

Let us go back to the *factorial* function, whose values we defined as follows:

$$factorial(1) = 1$$
$$factorial(2) = 2*1 \qquad = 2*factorial(1)$$
$$factorial(3) = 3*2*1 \qquad = 3*factorial(2)$$
$$factorial(4) = 4*3*2*1 \qquad = 4*factorial(3)$$

and so on. Note that

$factorial(1) = 1$
$factorial(2) = 2*factorial(2-1)$
$factorial(3) = 3*factorial(3-1)$
$factorial(4) = 4*factorial(4-1)$

We can summarize these results with the following two statements:

$factorial(1) = 1$
$factorial(n) = n*factorial (n-1)$

Here n stands for any integer greater than 1.

These two statements constitute a *recursive definition* of the *factorial* function, since the function is defined partly in terms of itself. Although defining something in terms of itself may sound paradoxical, we can easily see that the definition is a perfectly good one. For instance, suppose we want to compute the value of *factorial*(4). According to the recursive definition

$factorial(4) = 4*factorial(3)$

To find *factorial*(3) we use the definition again

$factorial(3) = 3*factorial(2)$

If we substitute the expression for *factorial*(3) on the right-hand side of the expression for *factorial*(4), we get

$factorial(4) = 4*3*factorial(2)$

But the recursive definition tells us that *factorial*(2) is defined by

$factorial(2) = 2*factorial(1)$

so

$factorial(4) = 4*3*2*factorial(1)$

Now, *factorial*(1) is *not* defined in terms of the *factorial* function. It is simply defined as having the value 1. Therefore, we can terminate the repeated uses of the definition and simply substitute 1 for *factorial*(1). This gives us

$factorial(4) = 4*3*2*1 = 24$

Thus recursion is a kind of repetition. To calculate a value for a function designator when the function is defined recursively, we must use the definition repeatedly. The repetition terminates when we arrive at a function designator whose value can be calculated without making use of the function being defined.

We want to write a version of the *factorial* function based on the recursive definition:

function *factorial* (*n*: *integer*): *integer*;
begin
    if *n* = 1 **then**
        factorial := 1
    else
        factorial := *n**factorial(*n*−1)
end

We must take care not to be confused by the fact that the identifier *factorial* is used in two different ways. When *factorial* appears on the left-hand side of the assignment operator, it refers to the memory location used to store the result the function returns. When *factorial* appears on the right-hand side of the assignment operator, it refers to the *factorial* function and causes a call to that function to take place.

Now let us see how the computer goes about executing the statement

i := *factorial*(5)

The *factorial* function is called with the actual parameter 5. In order for this function to calculate the result it is to return, it must execute

factorial := *n**factorial(*n*−1)

where the value of n is 5. Therefore the function *factorial* is called with the actual parameter 4. But in order for this invocation of *factorial* to do its calculations, it must call *factorial* with the actual parameter 3, and so on. Therefore, the following sequence of function calls takes place:

factorial(5)
factorial(4)
factorial(3)
factorial(2)
factorial(1)

Note that for each call a separate memory location named *n* has been set up. This is important because the value of *n* is different for each call, and these values will be needed to complete the calculations after the function calls start to return values.

Now *factorial* can return a value without doing any more function calls if the value of the actual parameter is 1. Therefore the value of *factorial*(1) is 1. This means that the function call *factorial*(2) can complete its calculations and return the value 2. But now *factorial*(3) can complete its calculations and return the value 6; and so on. The following shows the order in which the function calls return and the value that each returns:

factorial(1) = 1
factorial(2) = 2
factorial(3) = 6
factorial(4) = 24
factorial(5) = 120

Which of the two versions of the *factorial* function is best: the previous one that used the **for** statement or the recursive version? It turns out that the former version is best. The computer must take more time and use more memory setting up function calls and returns than for executing a **for**, **while**, or **repeat** statement.

So when a problem can be solved straightforwardly using one of the repetition statements, then that is the way it should be solved. There are, however, problems in which a recursive solution is straightforward and a repetitive one is complex and obscure; for these kinds of problems recursion is the preferred approach.

EXERCISES

For each of the following you should write not only the function or procedure called for, but a program that will "exercise" the function or procedure by providing it with data and printing the results that it produces.

1. Write a function

wages(*hours*, *rate*)

whose actual parameters are the hours a person worked and the amount per hour that the person is paid. The value of the function is the wages the person earns, with time-and-a-half for hours in excess of 40.

2. Write a function

maximum(*m*, *n*)

whose value is equal to the value of the largest of its two actual parameters.

3. Write a procedure

roll(*die1*, *die2*)

that assigns to *die1* and *die2* pseudorandom numbers in the range 1–6.

4. The value of

power(*m*, *n*)

is computed by starting with 1 and multiplying repeatedly by the value of *m*. The number of times one multiplies by the value of *m* is determined by the value of *n*. Thus:

power(3, 0) = 1
power(3, 1) = 1*3 = 3
power(3, 2) = 1*3*3 = 9
power(3, 3) = 1*3*3*3 = 27

and so on. Write the function *power*.

5. The function *power* can be defined recursively by the following statements:

power(*m*, 0) = 1
power(*m*, *n*) = *m**power(*m*, *n*−1)

Write a recursive version of the function *power*.

test 0 to see if you get 1

negative #'s

don't have to use this

power (x,n) = power (1/x - n)

0.5

If n<0 THEN

x:= 1/x; n:=-n;

Chapter 8

SIMPLE DATA TYPES

There are two aspects to computer programming: (1) the organization of the data that is to be processed, and (2) the statements that cause particular operations to be performed on the data. So far we have concentrated our attention on the statements that do the processing. With this chapter we will shift our attention toward the methods of organizing the data to be processed.

In Pascal, the organization of data is achieved by means of a system of data types. These data types are classified into *simple*, *structured*, and *pointer* types. The simple types are those whose values cannot be broken down into simpler components. The structured types are those whose values *can* be broken down into simpler components. The pointer types are those whose values are used to locate data items in the computer's memory.

We begin with the simple types, which are further subdivided into *scalar* and *subrange* types.

SCALAR DATA TYPES

The Standard Data Types

The four standard data types that we have been using all along

- *integer*
- *real*
- *Boolean*
- *char*

are scalar data types.

Data Type Definitions

Pascal allows the programmer to define new data types beyond the standard ones whose definitions are built into the language. We can illustrate the type-definition facility by looking at a rather trivial use of it. We can use type definitions to rename the standard data types. For instance, consider the following type definitions:

type
    fixed = *integer*;
    float = *real*;
    bit = *Boolean*;
    character = *char*;

       We could then declare

var
    i, j, k: fixed;
    x, y, z: float;
    p, q: bit;
    c: character;

When the Pascal machine processed these declarations, it would refer to the type definitions and act accordingly. Thus the possible values of *i*, *j*, and *k* would be the integers; the possible values of *x*, *y*, and *z* would be the real numbers; and so on.

   Data type definitions follow constant definitions and precede variable declarations at the beginning of a block. This is a good place to summarize the order in which the various definitions and declarations that we have taken up so far must occur:

- *constant definitions*
- *type definitions*
- *variable declarations*
- *function and procedure declarations*

Any of these definition or declaration parts that are not needed for a particular program can be omitted, of course. But those that are present have to be in the order shown.

User-Defined Scalar Types

Pascal allows the programmer to define new scalar data types by listing all the possible values of each type. The values of a user-defined type are represented by identifiers. For example, look at the following type definitions:

type
    day = (*sun, mon, tue, wed, thurs, fri, sat*);
    color = (*red, orange, yellow, green, blue, indigo, violet*);
    chessman = (*pawn, knight, bishop, rook, queen, king*);
    month = (*jan, feb, mar, apr, may, jun, july, aug, sept, oct, nov, dec*);
    grade = (*f, d, c, b, a*);

   If we declare a variable *d* by

var
    d: *day*

then the possible values of *d* are *sun, mon, tue,* and so on. Assignments such as

d := *mon*

or

d := *tue*

are possible.
   Note that the standard type *Boolean* could be defined by

Boolean = (*false, true*)

However, this definition is built into the Pascal machine and must not be supplied by the user.
   The same identifier may not be used for values of more than one type. Thus the definitions

rank = (*private, corporal, sergeant, lieutenant,*
              captain, major, colonel, general);
officer = (*lieutenant, captain, major, colonel, general*);

cannot both appear in the same program. The reason is that the types of *lieutenant, captain, major, colonel,* and *general* are not determined.

Operators and Functions on Scalar Data Types

All of the scalar data types are *ordered*. That is, the values of each type are assumed to occur in a certain order.
   For the standard data types, the order for integers and real numbers is the usual numerical order. For Boolean values the value *false* precedes the value

true. And for characters, the order is given by the collating sequence for the particular Pascal machine.

For user-defined scalar types, the order of the values is the order in which they are listed in the type definition. Thus for values of type *day*, *sun* precedes *mon*, *mon* precedes *tue*, and so on.

Since an order is defined for every scalar data type, the relational operators

$$= \quad < \quad > \quad <= \quad >= \quad <>$$

can be applied to values of any scalar type. (Both operands of the relational operator must be of the same type, however.) The following expressions illustrate the application of the relational operators to values of scalar types:

Expression	Value
sun < thurs	true
red >= blue	false
mar > apr	false
f = a	false
queen > rook	true

The functions *pred* and *succ* apply to values of all scalar types except *real*. *Pred* returns the value (if any) that immediately precedes the value of its actual parameter. *Succ* returns the value (if any) that immediately succeeds the value of its actual parameter.

For example, the following expressions illustrate the result of applying *pred* and *succ* to integer values:

Expression	Value
pred(5)	4
pred(4)	3
succ(5)	6
succ(6)	7

In fact, for integers $pred(i)$ has the same value as $i-1$ and $succ(i)$ has the same value as $i+1$. We do not need *pred* and *succ* for the integers since we can obtain the same effect using the more familiar expressions $i-1$ and $i+1$.

But for the *Boolean*, *char*, and user-defined scalar types, no arithmetic operations are defined, and so *pred* and *succ* serve useful purposes. The following are some expressions illustrating how *pred* and *succ* are used with these data types:

Expression	Value
succ(sun)	*mon*
pred(mon)	*sun*
pred(true)	*false*
succ(false)	*true*
pred('y')	*'x'*
succ('x')	*'y'*
succ(rook)	*queen*
pred(queen)	*rook*

The predecessor of the first value of a particular type and the successor of the last value are both undefined. Therefore, the values of the following expressions are not defined:

pred(false)
succ(true)
pred(sun)
succ(sat)
pred(pawn)
succ(king)
pred(jan)
succ(dec)
pred(f)
succ(a)

The values of a user-defined data type are considered to be numbered starting with 0 for the first value. For example, the values of type *day* are numbered as follows:

day = (*sun*, *mon*, *tue*, *wed*, *thurs*, *fri*, *sat*)
           0   1   2   3   4   5   6

The numbers are called the *ordinal numbers* of the corresponding values. Pascal has a standard function, *ord*, which returns the ordinal number of its actual parameter:

Expression	Value
ord(*sun*)	0
ord(*mon*)	1
ord(*tue*)	2
ord(*wed*)	3
.	
.	
.	
ord(*sat*)	6

The *ord* function can be applied to the standard types *Boolean* and *char* as well as to the user-defined scalar types. For *Boolean*, *ord*(*false*) equals 0 and *ord*(*true*) equals 1. For *char*, the ordinal numbers of the characters will vary from one Pascal machine to another just as the collating sequences do. The following examples assume the ASCII character set:

Expression	Value
ord('A')	65
ord('B')	66
ord('C')	67
ord('Z')	90
ord('0')	48
ord('9')	57

For the type *char* only, there is a function *chr* that converts an ordinal number back into the corresponding character:

Expression	Value
chr(65)	'A'
chr(90)	'Z'
chr(48)	'0'
chr(57)	'9'

Again the actual values used assume the ASCII code.

One use of the *chr* function is to obtain the nonprinting characters used for control purposes. For instance, in the ASCII code *chr*(7) is the *bell character*, which causes a terminal to ring a bell or make some other audible sound (electronic terminals usually beep rather than ring). The following procedure can be executed to bring some matter of importance to the user's attention:

```
procedure alarm;
const
    bell = 7; {in the ASCII code}
var
    i: integer;
begin
    for i := 1 to 10 do
        write(chr(bell))
end
```

Another important use of the *ord* and *chr* functions is to convert between the numerals '0' through '9' and the corresponding integers. The expression

$$ord(c) - ord('0')$$

converts the numeral that is the value of *c* to the corresponding integer:

Expression	Value
$ord('0') - ord('0')$	0
$ord('1') - ord('0')$	1
$ord('2') - ord('0')$	2
.	
.	
.	
$ord('9') - ord('0')$	9

To convert an integer in the range 0–9 to the corresponding numeral, we use the expression

$$chr(i + ord('0'))$$

which gives the following values:

Expression	Value
$chr(0 + ord('0'))$	'0'
$chr(1 + ord('0'))$	'1'
$chr(2 + ord('0'))$	'2'
.	
.	
.	
$chr(9 + ord('0'))$	'9'

The characters are the only data type for which a function is provided to convert ordinal numbers into the corresponding data values. However, we can easily write functions that will do this job for other data types. For instance, the following function *clr* converts a number from 0–6 into the corresponding color:

```
function clr(n: integer): color;
begin
    case n of
        0: clr := red;
        1: clr := orange;
        2: clr := yellow;
        3: clr := green;
        4: clr := blue;
        5: clr := indigo;
        6: clr := violet
    end
end
```

The data type *color* is assumed to be defined in the main program. In fact, global identifiers are much more commonly used with data types than with variables. It is common to define all the data types that a program will use in the main program. Since the type identifiers are then global, all the procedures and functions can make use of the defined types.

Using Scalar Types in for and case Statements

Any of the scalar data types except *real* can be used for the controlled variable in a **for** statement and the selector expression in a **case** statement. For example, if *d* is a variable of type *day*, then

```
for d := mon to fri do
    s1
```

causes the statement *s1* to be executed five times. The first time it is executed, the value of *d* is *mon*, the second time the value of *d* is *tue*, and so on.

The following statement will print a table of the uppercase letters and their ordinal numbers:

```
for c := 'A' to 'Z' do
    writeln(c, ord(c))
```

By executing statements of this form you can explore the character set that your computer uses.

The following statement illustrates the use of a variable *m* of type chessman as the selector in a **case** statement:

```
case m of
    pawn: s1;
    bishop: s2;
    knight: s3;
    rook: s4;
    queen: s5;
    king: s6
end
```

If the value of *m* is *pawn*, *s1* is executed; if the value of *m* is *bishop*, *s2* is executed; and so on.

SUBRANGE TYPES

For any scalar type except *real*, we can define a new type whose values are some subrange of the previously defined type. For instance,

digit = 0 . . 9;

defines a subrange of type *integer*,

workday = *mon . . fri*;

defines a subrange of type *day*, and

officer = *lieutenant . . general*;

defines a subrange of type *rank*.

The type whose values are used to define a subrange type is called the *associated scalar type*. All the operations that can be performed on the associated scalar type can also be performed on the subrange type. The only difference between the two types is that when a value is assigned to a variable of subrange type, then the Pascal machine checks to see that the value being assigned lies in the proper range. If it does not, the Pascal machine reports an error.

For instance, suppose *i* and *n* are declared as follows:

```
var
    i: integer;
    n: digit;
```

The assignment

i := *n*

is always valid, since a value of type *digit* is also a value of type *integer*. On the other hand, the assignment

$n := i$

is valid only if the value of *i* lies in the range 0–9. A value of type *integer* is also a value of type *digit*, but only if it lies in the range 0–9.

All the operations that can be carried out on integers can be carried out on digits as well. For instance, the statements

$n := 5;$
$n := n-3;$
$n := 2*n$

are valid (when executed in the order shown) since in every case the value assigned to *n* is a digit. On the other hand, consider the statements

$n := 7;$
$n := n+3$

After *n* is assigned the value 7, the value of $n+3$ is 10. When an attempt is made to assign this value to *n*, the Pascal machine reports an error.

As an example of the use of subrange types, the function *clr* could be improved by rewriting it as follows:

```
function clr(n: 0 . . 6): color;
begin
    case n of
        0: clr := red;
        1: clr := orange;
        2: clr := yellow;
        3: clr := green;
        4: clr := blue;
        5: clr := indigo;
        6: clr := violet
    end
end
```

must identify — TYPE

The use of the subrange type 0 . . 6 in declaring the formal parameter makes it clear to someone reading the program that a call on this function is meaningful only if the value of its actual parameter is in the range 0–6. Also, when the function is actually called, the computer checks that the actual parameter is indeed in this range and reports the error if it is not. For a function this simple such checking may not be of overwhelming importance, but it would be much more important for a more complicated function where an actual parameter out of range could cause hard-to-diagnose problems.

Notice that in this example the subrange type 0..6 was used directly in the formal parameter declaration without first naming it in a type definition. This is always possible. Thus instead of defining types *day* and *digit* and declaring *d* and *n* by

var
    d: *day*;
    n: *digit*;

we could just as well have declared *d* and *n* directly by

var
    d: (*sun*, *mon*, *tue*, *wed*, *thurs*, *fri*, *sat*);
    n: 0 . . 9;

There are two reasons for introducing type identifiers. One is for documentation—to let us give the type a descriptive name that suggests its use in the program. The other is so that the type identifier can be used in functions and procedures to declare formal parameters and local variables to be of the same type as some variable in the main program.

EXERCISES

1. Write a program to print the alphabet as follows:

ABCDEFGHIJKLMNOPQRSTUVWXYZ

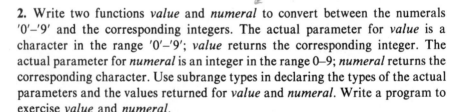

2. Write two functions *value* and *numeral* to convert between the numerals '0'–'9' and the corresponding integers. The actual parameter for *value* is a character in the range '0'–'9'; *value* returns the corresponding integer. The actual parameter for *numeral* is an integer in the range 0–9; *numeral* returns the corresponding character. Use subrange types in declaring the types of the actual parameters and the values returned for *value* and *numeral*. Write a program to exercise *value* and *numeral*.

3. The procedures *read* and *readln* will not read the values of user-defined data types from cards or computer terminals. We must write procedures to do this job. Suppose values of type *day* are typed in as follows:

M _   T _   W _   TH   F _   S _   SU

The underlines represent blank spaces. Write a function that reads two characters and returns the corresponding value of type *day*.

Chapter 9

STRUCTURED TYPES: ARRAYS

A structured data type, you remember, is one whose values are each made up of simpler component values. Different methods of organizing the component values give rise to different structured data types.

/ One way of organizing values is to arrange them in lists or tables. The structured data types that use this method of organization are known as *array types* or, more simply, as *arrays*.

ONE-DIMENSIONAL ARRAYS

We can think of a one-dimensional array as a *list* of values. For a definite example, let us consider a list of five integers, such as the following:

(1) 25

(2)   4

(3) 39

(4) 17

(5)   2

The values on the list are 25, 4, 39, 17, and 2. The integers 1 through 5 at the left are known as *indices*. Their purpose is to provide us with a convenient way of referring to the individual *components** of the list. For instance, we can see at once that component number 3 is 39 and component number 5 is 2.

The data type whose values are the kind of lists just described is defined in Pascal as follows:

type
  list = **array**[1 . . 5] **of** *integer*;

This definition mentions two data types. The type mentioned in parentheses is the *index type*. It is the type whose values will be used to label the components of the array. Here the index type is the subrange type 1 . . 5, which tells us that the components of a value of type *list* will be labeled with the values 1 through 5.

The other data type, the one that follows the word **of**, is called the *component type*. As the name implies, it is the type of the components of a value of type *list*.

Now suppose we declare some variables to be of type *list*:

var
   a, b: *list*;

Each of the identifiers *a* and *b* must name a memory location capable of holding five integers. For the variable *a* we could diagram this situation as follows:

a

| 25 |
| 4 |
| 39 |
| 17 |
| 2 |

Only the components of the array are stored. The index values are not needed, since the components are stored in such a way that the Pascal machine can locate the component corresponding to any index value.

Now, since the memory location named *a* can hold five integer values, this memory location must be made up of five smaller locations, each of which can hold a single integer value. That is, the memory location *a* has a structure that mirrors structure of the values that can be assigned to it. The following diagram shows the subdivision of the location *a* into five locations, each of which holds a single integer:

---

* The components of an array are also frequently referred to as the *elements* of the array.

a	25
	4
	39
	17
	2

When we store a list in memory our reasons for doing so are to use the values on the list, to store new values on the list, or (usually) both. Therefore, we need some way of referring to the memory locations that hold the individual components of the list.

We do this by placing the index of the component we wish to refer to in brackets after the name of the location that holds the entire list. Thus $a[1]$ names the memory location that holds the first component of the value of a, $a[2]$ names the memory location that holds the second component of the value of a, and so on. We can diagram this situation as follows:

$a[1]$	25
$a[2]$	4
$a[3]$	39
$a[4]$	17
$a[5]$	2

The variable a whose value is the entire array is known as an *array variable*. The variables $a[1]$, $a[2]$, $a[3]$, $a[4]$ and $a[5]$, whose values are the components of the array, are known as *indexed variables*.

Indexed variables can be used in any of the ways that are permissible for the variables we have discussed previously. For instance, they can be used on the left-hand sides of assignment statements. The statements

$a[1] := 95;$
$a[3] := 71;$
$a[5] := 11$

change the value of a as follows:

a	95
	4
	71
	17
	11

Notice that the only values changed were those of the indexed variables that appeared on the left-hand sides of assignment statements.

Indexed variables can also be used in expressions. For instance, if the statements

$i := a[1] - a[2]$;
$j := 2*a[3]$
$k := a[4]*a[5]$

are now executed, the variables i, j, and k are assigned the values

Variable	Value
i	91
j	142
k	187

Also, the statement

$writeln(a[1], a[2], a[3], a[4], a[5])$

causes the computer to print

95   4   71   17   11

The index type can be any simple data type other than real or integer. The most commonly used index types are the subranges of the integers. However *Boolean*, *char*, and user-defined scalar types can also be used as index types. For example, recall the types *day* and *chessman* defined in the previous chapter:

type
    day = (*sun, mon, tue, wed, thurs, fri, sat*);
    chessman = (*pawn, bishop, knight, rook, queen, king*);

The following arrays use these types as index types:

var
    hours: **array**[*day*] **of** *real*;
    value: **array**[*chessman*] **of** *integer*;

The indexed variables corresponding to the array variable *hours* are

hours[*sun*]   *hours*[*mon*]   *hours*[*tue*]   *hours*[*wed*]
hours[*thurs*]   *hours*[*fri*]   *hours*[*sat*]

These can be used to record the number of hours that an employee worked each day of the week. For instance,

hours[*mon*] := 7.4

would record the fact that the employee worked 7.4 hours on Monday.

We could use the array *value* to record the relative values of the different kinds of chessmen:

value[*pawn*] := 1; *value*[*bishop*] := 3;
value[*knight*] := 3; *value*[*rook*] := 5;
value[*queen*] := 9; *value*[*king*] := 1000

(Although the king is theoretically priceless, the needs of chess-playing programs are often best served by assigning the king a large but finite value.)

In a chess-playing program, each side is usually given a material score, which represents the sum of the values of all that side's chessmen. If *ms* is the material score for a particular side, and that side loses its queen, then its material score is updated as follows:

ms := *ms* − *value*[*queen*]

When variables were first introduced, it was pointed out that we would often use shorthand statements such as "*i* equals 25" and "*n* is the number of items to be processed." Our purpose was to avoid the more precise but clumsier versions, "the value of the variable *i* is 25" and "the value of the variable *n* is the number of items to be processed."

Let us try to achieve a similar simplification in the terminology of arrays. Strictly speaking, a variable such as *list*, which we introduced at the beginning of this section, is an *array variable*, and its value (the list of numbers) is the *array*. For simplicity, however, we will often use the term *array* for both variable and value, letting the context show which is meant in each case.

Also, we will often use the indexed variables *list*[1], *list*[2], *list*[3], and so on as names for the components of the value of *list*. Thus we will say "*list*[1] equals 25" instead of "the value of the indexed variable *list*[1] is 25" or "the first component of the value of *list* is 25."

USING ONE-DIMENSIONAL ARRAYS

Arrays and for Statements

Arrays and **for** statements work very well together. The **for** statement steps the value of a variable through a series of index values, thereby allowing the corresponding components of an array to be referred to.

For instance, let us add up the values of the array *a* using the integer variable *sum*:

sum := 0;
for *i* := 1 **to** 5 **do**
    sum := *sum*+*a*[*i*];

These are equivalent to the following six statements:

sum := 0;
sum := *sum*+*a*[1];
sum := *sum*+*a*[2];
sum := *sum*+*a*[3];
sum := *sum*+*a*[4];
sum := *sum*+*a*[5]

This example illustrates an important property of arrays. The index does not have to be a constant; it can be any expression that yields a value of the index type. Therefore, we do not have to specify the value of the index when we write the program; the value can be computed as the program executes. For instance, the value of the index might depend on the data that the program inputs. Or, as in the case of the statement

sum := *sum*+*a*[*i*]

we can write a statement once but use it many times, each time with a different value for the index.

Here is another example. Suppose we want to find the smallest and largest components of an array. For instance, the components of the array might be the temperatures recorded on a particular day, and we might want to find the high and the low for the day. Let *high*, *low*, and *temp* be declared as follows:

var
    high, *low*: *integer*;
    temp: **array**[1 .. 24] **of** *integer*;

We start by setting both *high* and *low* to the value of *temp*[1]. Then, starting with the value of *temp*[2], we go through the array and compare each component with the values of *high* and *low*. When a component is found to be greater than the value of *high*, then that component becomes the new value of *high*. When a component is found to be less than the value of *low*, then that component becomes the new value of *low*:

low := *temp*[1];
high := *temp*[1];
for *i* := 2 **to** 24 **do**
    if *temp*[*i*] > *high* **then** {*we found a new high*}
        high := *temp*[*i*]
    else if *temp*[*i*] < *low* **then** {*we found a new look*}
        low := *temp*[*i*]

Arrays can be used as actual parameters for procedures and functions. (However, arrays and other structured types cannot be returned as the values of functions.) For instance, we could write a procedure to compute the high and low temperatures:

```
procedure extremes (var low, high: integer;
                    var temp: array[1 . . 24] of integer);
var
    i: integer;
begin
    low := temp[1];
    high :=temp[1];
    for i := 2 to 24 do
        if temp[i] > high then
            high := temp[i]
        else if temp[i] < low then
            low := temp[i]
end
```

Notice that we have made the array a variable parameter even though it is not used to return values to the calling program. This is done for the sake of efficiency. If we had made the array a value parameter, then all 24 components would have had to be copied into the procedure's private memory area. For 24 components this would not be too bad, but what if we were dealing with an array with 1000 components? Then a considerable amount of time could be spent just copying components into the procedure's memory area. By making the array a variable parameter, the procedure is given access to the array stored in the calling program's memory area, and no copying takes place.

As an example of a function with an array as a parameter, let us write a function that finds the average of an array of real numbers:

TYPE   List = ARRAY [1 . . 100] of real

```
function average(var a: array[1 . . 100] of real; count: integer): real;
var
    i: integer;
    sum: real;
begin
    sum := 0.0;
    for i := 1 to count do
        sum := sum+a[i];
    average := sum/count
end
```

The value of the parameter *count* is the number of values to be averaged. It might seem that this should always be 100, since the array *a* has 100 components. However, an array is often declared for the largest number of components that might be needed for any possible use of the program. For any particular execution of the program fewer components may be needed. Hence the actual number of elements to be averaged must be passed to the function. This function will work correctly for values of *count* in the range 1–100.

An array used as an actual parameter must be of the same type as the corresponding formal parameter—it must have the same index type and the same component type. Thus the array that is substituted for the formal parameter *a* in *average* must have the type

array[1 . . 100] **of** *real*

Array Assignment

Most operators do not act on arrays as a whole but on their components—the values of the indexed variables. However, if *a* and *b* are any two array variables *of the same type* (same index type, same component type), the assignment operator can be used to assign the value of one array variable to the other.

For instance, suppose that *a* and *b* are declared by

var
    a, *b*: **array**[1 . . 5] **of** *integer*;

Then the statement

a := *b*

is equivalent to the five statements

a[1] := *b*[1];
a[2] := *b*[2];
a[3] := *b*[3];
a[4] := *b*[4];
a[5] := *b*[5]

If before the assignment the values of *a* and *b* are

a		*b*	
	21		14
	10		95
	5		30
	87		61
	52		11

then after the assignment their values are

a		*b*	
	14		14
	95		95
	30		30
	61		61
	11		11

Input and Output of Arrays

Arrays are read in and written out component by component. Fortunately, we can use a **for** statement to read and write as many components as needed.

For instance, the statement

for $i := 1$ **to** 5 **do**
   $read(a[i])$

reads five values and assigns them to $a[1]$ through $a[5]$. If the data is

17   29   14   38   75

then 17 is assigned to $a[1]$, 29 to $a[2]$, 14 to $a[3]$, and so on.

Printing is handled the same way. For instance, if the statement

for $i := 1$ **to** 5 **do**
   $write(a[i]:4)$

is now executed, the computer prints:

17   29   14   38   75

If we want the values to be printed vertically instead of horizontally, we can use

for $i := 1$ **to** 5 **do**
   $writeln(a[i])$

and get the printout

17
29
14
38
75

If a particular type of array has to be read in or printed out in many different parts of a program, we can write procedures to do the reading and printing.

```
procedure read5(var h: array[1 . . 5] of integer);
var
    i: integer;
begin
    for i := 1 to 5 do
        read(h[i]);
end;
```

```
procedure write5(var h: array [1 . . 5] of integer);
var
    i: integer;
begin
    for i := 1 to 5 do
        write(h[i]:4)
end
```

With these procedures, we can read the value of the array *a* with the statement

read5(*a*)

and write the value of *a* with the statement

write5(*a*)

Translation Tables

In the previous chapter we defined the type *color* by

```
type
    color = (red, orange, yellow, green, blue, indigo, violet);
```

and wrote a function *clr* to translate an ordinal number in the range 0–6 into the corresponding color. This translation can be done more simply and more efficiently by using an array.

Let us declare the array *t* by

```
var
    t: array[0 . . 6] of color;
```

and assign to its components values as follows:

```
t[0] := red;      t[1] := orange;
t[2] := yellow;   t[3] := green;
t[4] := blue;     t[5] := indigo;
t[6] := violet
```

Now, if the value of *i* is any integer in the range 0–6, then the value of

t[*i*]

is the corresponding color—the color that has the value of *i* as its ordinal number. As a rule the computer can determine the value of *t*[*i*] much more quickly than it can call and execute the function that was given in the previous chapter.

With the aid of *t* we can represent a color in two different ways: (1) an integer in the range 0–6; (2) a value of type *color*. The standard function *ord* translates values from type *color* to type $0..6$. The array *t* translates values from type $0..6$ to type *color*. For this reason *t* is sometimes called a *translation table*.

It is not uncommon in large programs to have to represent the same information in different ways (that is, using values of different types) in different parts of the program. When this has to be done, arrays come in very handy for translating from one representation to another.

Packed Arrays

Any array type can be preceded by the reserved word **packed**, as in

packed array$[1..5]$ **of** *Boolean*

The word **packed** instructs the Pascal machine to store the values of the array in memory in as compact a manner as possible, even if this means packing more than one value into each memory location.

The advantage of a packed array is, of course, that it takes up less memory space than one that is not packed. On the other hand, the computer usually takes longer to access a component of a packed array, since it not only has to access the memory location containing the desired value, it also has to isolate that value from the others sharing the same memory location.

The types of arrays that are most commonly packed are arrays of *char* and *Boolean*. Often *char* and *Boolean* values take up only a small part of a memory location, so storing more than one value per location saves considerable space. Also, arrays of subrange types can be packed effectively, since the computer requires less memory to store values of type $0..7$, say, than to store values of type *integer*.

Whether or not values of a particular type should be packed depends on how those values are represented inside your Pascal machine. The amount of memory saved in packing a particular type of array, and the time lost in accessing its components, will vary considerably from one Pascal machine to another.

Packed arrays can be referenced just like any other arrays. Thus if *pc* is declared by

var
    pc: **packed array**$[1..5]$ **of** *char*;

then the references

$c := pc[3]$;
$pc[5] := \text{'A'}$

are valid.

However, for the reasons that have been mentioned, repeated references to a packed array may be time consuming. In many cases it is less time consuming to pack or unpack the entire array at once, instead of referring repeatedly to packed values. For this reason Pascal provides two procedures, *pack* and *unpack*, for packing and unpacking an entire array at once.

To see how these procedures work, consider the array variables a and z declared as follows:

var
    a: **array**[1 . . 10] **of** *char*;
    z: **packed array**[1 . . 7] **of** *char*;

Then the statement

pack(*a, 3, z*)

causes the values of $a[3]$ through $a[9]$ to be packed into z. That is, this statement accomplishes the same result

for $i := 1$ **to** 7 **do**
    $z[i] := a[i+2]$

Going in the reverse direction, the statement

unpack(*z, a, 3*)   *where you want to begin with the packed elements; a from z*

causes the value of z to be unpacked and its components to be stored in $a[3]$ through $a[9]$. This statement accomplishes the same result as would

for $i := 1$ **to** 7 **do**
    $a[i+2] := z[i]$

Notice that the size of the packed array determines the number of values that will be packed or unpacked.

Packed Arrays of Characters

We have been using string constants such as 'hello' all along but so far have not talked about a string data type. In most versions of Pascal strings are defined as packed arrays of characters. Thus, 'hello' is a constant of type

packed array[1 . . 5] **of** *char*

and 'goodbye' is a constant of type

packed array[1 . . 7] **of** *char*

Packed arrays of characters are the only array types for which array constants are provided. For all other types of arrays, constant values must be assigned component by component.

Suppose we have an array variable *name* declared by

name: **packed array**[1 . . 10] **of** *char*;

We can use string constants to assign values to *name*. But we must be careful—the assignment operator only works when the arrays on the left and right are of the same type. Therefore, any string constant used to assign values to *name* must contain exactly 10 characters. If the value we wish to assign has fewer than 10 characters, then we must pad it out to ten characters by adding blank spaces. For instance, the following are possible assignments to *name*:

name := 'John   '
name := 'Bill   '
name := 'Robert   '
name := 'Jackson   '
name := 'Harrington'

Note that in each case enough blanks have been added to the right of the name to make up the 10 characters needed.

Pascal provides two special considerations for packed arrays of characters. First, the relational operators can be applied to packed arrays of characters of the same type and will compare them for alphabetical order (where alphabetical order is defined by the collating sequence for the Pascal machine). Thus the following Boolean expressions are all valid and all have the value *true*:

'JACK' < 'JOHN'
'BILL' < 'MARY'
'BUD' > 'BOB'
'JOHNSON' > 'JACKSON'

When one of the strings contains blanks, then the result depends on where the blank comes in the collating sequence. In the ASCII character set (and many others as well), the blank comes before any of the numerals or the letters of the alphabet. In this case, the following expressions all yield the value *true* (the blanks are underlined to make them visible):

'BILL _ ' < 'BILLY'
'JACK _ _ _ ' < 'JACKSON'
'TOGETHER _ _ _ _ ' < 'TOGETHERNESS'

The second special consideration that Pascal provides to packed arrays of characters is that when a variable of this type appears in a *write* or *writeln* statement, the entire array is written out. Indeed, we have made use of this feature when we used write statements such as

writeln('Sales Tax: ', *salestax*:6:2)

Here the string constant

'Sales Tax: '

is an array of type

packed array[1 . . 11] **of** *char*

This string could be represented just as well by the value of an array variable. For instance, if we declare

message: **packed array**[1 . . 11] **of** *char*;

and assign

message := 'Sales Tax: '

then the two statements

writeln(*message*, *salestax*:6:2)

and

writeln('Sales Tax: ', *salestax*:6:2)

produce the same printout.

No assistance is provided for reading packed arrays of characters, which must be read character by character. To read in a ten-character name, for instance, we can use

for *i* := 1 **to** 10 **do**
   read(*name*[*i*])

We could avoid the inefficiency of accessing components of a packed array by declaring

nm: **array**[1 . . 10] **of** *char*;

and executing the following:

for *i* := 1 **to** 10 **do**
   read(*nn*[*i*]);
pack(*nm*, 1, *name*)

In most cases the time saved with this method is insignificant, and the simpler method can be used.

Using packed arrays of characters we can modify some of our previous programs to read and print people's names instead of just their ID numbers. We can do this for the program *payroll*, for instance:

program *payroll3*(*input*, *output*);
type
   empname = **packed array**[1 . . 20] **of** *char*;
var
   employee: *empname*;
   hours, *rate*, *wages*: *real*;

```
procedure getname(var n: empname);
var
    i: integer;
begin
    for i := 1 to 20 do
        read(n[i])
end; {of getname}


begin {main program}
    writeln('Employee                    ', 'Hours':10, 'Rate':10, 'Wages':10);
    writeln;
    while not eof(input) do
        begin
            getname(employee);
            readln(hours, rate);
            if hours > 40.0 then
                wages := 40.0*rate + 1.5*rate*(hours−40.0)
            else
                wages := rate*hours;
            writeln(employee, hours:10:1, rate:10:2, wages:10:2)
        end
end.
```

In the data for this program, it is essential that each name be followed by enough blank spaces to make up 20 characters.

THE CHANGE-MAKING PROGRAM

Now let us write a somewhat more elaborate program using arrays. This program will input an amount of change and print the number of each type of bill and coin that must be handed back to make up the given amount of change. For instance, if the amount of change is 26.37, then the program will print the following list of bills and coins to be returned:

Twenties	1
Tens	0
Fives	1
Ones	1
Halves	0
Quarters	1
Dimes	1
Nickels	0
Pennies	2

To begin with, we have to store the names of the bills and coins in a form we can easily print out. Since the strings 'Twenties' and 'Quarters' are the longest, with eight characters each, we can define a data type *denomination* for the demoninations of the bills and coins:

denomination = **packed array**[1 . . 8] **of** *char*;

We need to coordinate two kinds of information: the names of the bills and coins, and their values in cents. We can do this with two arrays, *names* and *values*:

names: **array**[1 . . 9] **of** *denomination*;
values: **array**[1 . . 9] **of** *integer*;

For each value of *i* in the range 1–9, *names*[*i*] gives the name of a particular bill or coin and *values*[*i*] gives the value of the bill or coin in cents. Arrays used in this way are often referred to as *parallel arrays*, since we can think of the components of one as being written down side-by-side (in parallel with) the components of the other:

names	values
'Twenties '	2000
'Tens '	1000
'Fives '	500
'Ones '	100
'Halves '	50
'Quarters '	25
'Dimes '	10
'Nickels '	5
'Pennies '	1

Using parallel arrays to set up a correspondence between two sets of values is a common practice in computer programming.

As to the calculation of the change itself, suppose the amount of change to be returned in dollars and cents is read by

read(*amount*)

where *amount* is a real variable. The number of cents that must be returned is given by

change := *round*(100.0*amount*)

where *change* is an integer variable.

You may wonder why *round* is used here instaed of *trunc*. The reason is this: On computers that use the binary number system, common decimal fractions such as 0.10 are not represented accurately inside the computer. Thus the amount 35.10 might be stored as the binary equivalent of

35.099999999

The expression

trunc(100.0*35.099999999)

has the value 3509, which is a penny short. However, the value of

round(100.0*35.099999999)

is 3510, which is the desired answer.

Suppose that the value of *change* is the number of cents that have not yet been returned to the customer. To find out how many of a particular denomination of bill or coin we must return, we divide *change* by the value of the bill or coin in cents. For instance, the number of dimes that should be returned is the value of

change **div** 10

The remainder of this division,

change **mod** 10

is the number of cents that remain to be handed back after the dimes have been handed out. For instance, if the value of *change* is 27 cents, then we have

$$
\begin{array}{r}
2 \\
10{\overline{\smash{\big)}\,27}} \\
\underline{20} \\
7
\end{array}
\quad
\begin{array}{l}
(27 \textbf{ div } 10) \\
\\
\\
(27 \textbf{ mod } 10)
\end{array}
$$

The customer receives two dimes, and seven cents still remain to be handed back.

Now the value in cents of a particular bill or coin is *values*[*i*], where the value of *i* determines the bill or coin to which we are referring. The number of the bill or coin that should be handed back is

change **div** *values*[*i*]

The value of *change* is then updated to the number of cents that still remain to be handed back:

change := *change* **mod** *value*[*i*]

The calculations just given can now be repeated using the new value of *change* and the next value of *i*.

These ideas lead to the following program:

```
program change(input, output);
type
    denomination = packed array[1 . . 8] of char;
var
    names: array[1 . . 9] of denomination;
    values: array[1 . . 9] of integer;
    amount: real;
    change, i: integer;
begin
    names[1] := 'Twenties ';      values[1] := 2000;
    names[2] := 'Tens     ';      values[2] := 1000;
    names[3] := 'Fives    ';      values[3] :=  500;
    names[4] := 'Ones     ';      values[4] :=  100;
    names[5] := 'Halves   ';      values[5] :=   50;
    names[6] := 'Quarters ';      values[6] :=   25;
    names[7] := 'Dimes    ';      values[7] :=   10;
    names[8] := 'Nickels  ';      values[8] :=    5;
    names[9] := 'Pennies  ';      values[9] :=    1;
    while not eof(input) do
        begin
            readln(amount);
            writeln('Amount to be returned is ', amount:6:2);
            writeln;
            change := round(100.0*amount);
            for i := 1 to 9 do
                begin
                    writeln(names[i], (change div values[i]):4);
                    change := change mod values[i]
                end;
            writeln;
            writeln
        end
end.
```

MULTIDIMENSIONAL ARRAYS

The arrays we have discussed so far are called *one-dimensional* arrays, since they only extend in one dimension—up and down the page. Sometimes we need tables in which the values extend in two dimensions—across the page as well as up and down. These tables are called *two-dimensional arrays*.

We can declare a two-dimensional array in Pascal as follows:

```
t: array[1 . . 4, 1 . . 3] of integer;
```

The array *t* is a table of integers with four rows and three columns. The rows are labeled with the index values 1 through 4; the columns are labeled with the index values 1 through 3. For the sake of a definite example, let us assume that the value of *t* is as follows:

t

	1	2	3
1	17	30	25
2	14	18	65
3	19	50	24
4	75	96	80

The integers on the left are the row indices and those at the top are the column indices. We can specify any position in the table by giving a row index and a column index. Thus, the value 65 is at the intersection of row 2 and column 3; the value 19 is at the intersection of row 3 and column 1; and so on. As was the case with one-dimensional arrays, the index values do not have to be stored in the computer's memory.

Also as was the case with one-dimensional arrays, we can use indexed variables to refer to the components of a two-dimensional array. Two indices are required; the first of these is the row index, and the second is the column index. Thus *t*[3, 2] refers to the component in the third row and second column of *t*; its value is 50. The indexed variable *t*[1, 2] refers to the component in the first row and second column of *t*; its value is 30. In the same way, *t*[*i*, *j*] refers to the component in the row determined by the value of *i* and the column determined by the value of *j*.

The *dimensions* of an array refer to the number of indices required to specify a particular component. Thus a one-dimensional array requires one index; a two-dimensional array requires two; a three-dimensional array requires three; and so on. Pascal places no limit on the dimensions of arrays, so arrays of three and higher dimensions are allowed.

As an example of a three-dimensional array, consider the following:

b: **array**[1 . . 30, 1 . . 5, 1 . . 4] **of** *integer*;

One way to think of *b* is as a *book of tables*. The first index specifies a page in the book, the second specifies a row in the table on the selected page; and the third specifies a column in the same table. Thus, *b*[12, 3, 2] refers to the value found in the table on page 12 at the intersection of row 3 and column 2; *b*[25, 4, 3] refers to the value found in the table on page 25 at the intersection of row 4 and column 3.

Using Two-Dimensional Arrays

Let us look at a typical application of two-dimensional arrays. Suppose we are processing the data from a political poll. There are three candidates running—Johnson, Roberts, and Saxon. The voters we are questioning are of three political persuasions—Democrat, Republican, and Independent. We are interested in finding the number of people of each political persuasion who are for each candidate.

Suppose each voter questioned is asked for his or her political party and candidate preference. The results of the poll can be summarized as follows:

	Johnson	Roberts	Saxon
Democrat	253	40	98
Republican	75	370	150
Independent	24	107	228

That is, of all the Democrats questioned, 253 were for Johnson, 40 were for Roberts, and 98 were for Saxon. Of all the Republicans questioned, 75 were for Johnson, 370 were for Roberts, and so on.

We can use a three-by-three array, *count*, to store this data. The array variable *count* is declared as follows:

count: **array**[1 . . 3, 1 . . 3] **of** *integer*;

Thus the value of *count*[1, 3] is the number of Democrats for Saxon, the value of *count*[3, 2] is the number of Independents for Roberts, and so on.

We will use the index values as codes for the parties and the candidates. Thus in our data we will code the three parties and the three candidates as follows:

Party	Code	Candidate	Code
Democrat	1	Johnson	1
Republican	2	Roberts	2
Independent	3	Saxon	3

Suppose we code the raw data obtained when the poll is taken as follows. Two integers are recorded for each person questioned. The first integer is the code for the person's party and the second integer is the code for the candidate the person prefers. Thus the data

2   1

represents a Republican who prefers Johnson, and

1   3

represents a Democrat who prefers Saxon.

Now let us write a procedure to input data of this type, and to record in *count* the number of people with each particular party affiliation and candidate preference.

Before starting to input data, all the entries in *count* must be set to 0. We can do this as follows: The statement

$$count[i, j] := 0$$

sets to zero the component of *count* determined by the values of *i* and *j*. If the statement just given is repeated with *j* taking on the values 1, 2, and 3

for *j* := 1 **to** 3 **do**
   count[*i*, *j*] := 0

then the row of *count* determined by the value of *i* is set to 0. If the last statement is repeated with *i* taking on the values 1, 2, and 3

for *i* := 1 **to** 3 **do**
  for *j* := 1 **to** 3 **do**
    count[*i*, *j*] := 0

then all the components of the array are set to 0. Notice that we have here an example of *nested* **for** *statements*—one **for** statement is contained within another. Nested **for** statements occur frequently in working with arrays of dimension two or higher.

The data for each person questioned is processed as follows:

readln(*p*, *c*);
count[*p*, *c*] := *count*[*p*, *c*] + 1

where *p* and *c* are variables of type 1 . . 3, a subrange of *integer*. The computer reads the party affiliation (the value of *p*) and the candidate preference (the value of *c*) for a particular person and adds 1 to the appropriate component of *count* (*count*[*p*, *c*]). The procedure *getdata* reads the data and counts the number of people with each party affiliation and candidate preference:

```
procedure getdata;
var
    p, c: 1 . . 3;
begin
    for p := 1 to 3 do
        for c := 1 to 3 do
            count[p, c] := 0;
    while not eof(input) do
        begin
            readln(p, c);
            count[p, c] := count[p, c] + 1
        end
end
```

Here we assume that *count* is a global variable. Remember we have said before that one use of global variables is to hold data that will be manipulated by a number of procedures. *Count* is a good example of this.

Having obtained the entries in *count* one thing we are interested in doing is printing those values out. To see what statements we need, we can reason much as we did with the statements that set the entries in *count* to 0. The statement

write(count[p, c]:15)

prints the component of *count* determined by the values of *p* and *c*. By repeating this statement with *c* taking on the values 1, 2, and 3, we can print a row of *count*:

for *c* := 1 **to** 3 **do**
   write(count[p, c]:15)

After we have finished one row, we want the computer to go to a new line of printout, so that the different rows of *count* will be printed on different lines. This can be done by putting a *writeln* statement after the statement that prints a row.

for *c* := 1 **to** 3 **do**
   write(count[p, c]:15);
writeln

To get all three rows of *count* printed, execute the above statements for *p* equal to 1, 2, and 3:

for *p* := 1 **to** 3 **do**
  begin
     for *c* := 1 **to** 3 **do**
       write(count[p, c]:15);
     writeln
  end

For the sample data previously given, these statements produce the following printout:

```
253          40          98
 75         370         150
 24         107         228
```

This printout, however, is a bit cryptic unless one already knows the party corresponding to each row, and the candidate corresponding to each column. Is there some way we can print out the names of the candidates and the parties as well?

Printing the names of the candidates is no problem:

writeln('Johnson':26, 'Roberts':15, 'Saxon':15)

(The reason for using a field width of 26 for Johnson is to leave the room for the column that contains the party affiliations.)

To get the party affiliation printed for each row is a bit more difficult. Let us declare a global array variable *parties* as follows:

type
    party = **packed array**[1 . . 11] **of** *char*;
var
    parties: **array**[1 . . 3] **of** *party*;

At the beginning of the main program, we give the components of *parties* values as follows:

parties[1] :=   'Democrat   ';
parties[2] :=   'Republican ';
parties[3] :=   'Independent'

Before beginning to print each row of *count* we execute

write(parties[p])

to print the party affiliation. The following procedure prints the components of *count* along with the names of the parties and candidates:

```
procedure putdata;
var
    p, c: 1 . . 3;
begin
    writeln('Johnson':26, 'Roberts':15, 'Saxon':15);
    writeln;
    for p := 1 to 3 do
        begin
            write(parties[p]);
            for c := 1 to 3 do
                write(count[p, c]:15);
            writeln
        end
end
```

Let us look at some of the other things we might want to do with the data in *count*. For instance, we might want to add up all the entries to get the total number of people questioned. Of course, we could have gotten this total when the data for count was read by counting the number of data entries. But we want to see how to add up the components of a two-dimensional array, so we will do the computation this way.

Let *total* be an integer variable. We start out setting the value of *total* to 0. Then we add the value of each component of *count* to the value of *total*. The statements that do this have a form that will be familiar by now:

```
total := 0;
for p := 1 to 3 do
    for c := 1 to 3 do
        total := total+count[p, c]
```

One thing that obviously interests us is the total number of people for each candidate. Let us declare an array variable *ctotal* to hold these totals:

```
ctotal: array[1 . . 3] of integer;
```

Thus *ctotal*[1] is the total number of people who favor Johnson, *ctotal*[2] is the total number of people who favor Roberts, and *ctotal*[3] is the total number of people who favor Saxon.

To compute the total for the column corresponding to the index *c*, we use:

```
ctotal[c] := 0;
for p := 1 to 3 do
    ctotal[c] := ctotal[c]+count[p, c]
```

To get the totals for all three candidates, we need to execute these statements for *c* equal to 1, 2, and 3:

```
for c := 1 to 3 do
    begin
        ctotal[c] := 0;
        for p := 1 to 3 do
            ctotal[c] := ctotal[c]+count[p, c]
    end
```

Another set of totals we might want is the total number of people questioned who belong to each party. For instance, the totals for the candidates might not be very meaningful if the proportions of people belonging to each party in the group questioned are not the same as in the population at large.

Let us use an array *ptotal* for the party totals:

```
ptotal: array[1 . . 3] of integer;
```

Then *ptotal*[1] is the number of Democrats questioned, and so on.

To compute the total for the row corresponding to the value of *p*, we use:

```
ptotal[p] := 0;
for c := 1 to 3 do
    ptotal[p] := ptotal[p]+count[p, c]
```

To get the totals for all three parties, we repeat these statements for *p* equal to 1, 2, and 3:

```
for p := 1 to 3 do
    begin
        ptotal[p] := 0;
        for c := 1 to 3 do
            ptotal[p] := ptotal[p]+count[p, c]
    end
```

EXERCISES

1. Write a version of the program *grades* (Chapter 6) in which the letter grade corresponding to a particular score is computed using

grade := *lettergrade*[*score* **div** 10]

where *lettergrade* is an array variable declared by

lettergrade: **array**[0 . . 10] **of** *char*;

2. Modify the program *change* so that the change for 13.46 is printed as follows:

one	ten
three	ones
one	quarter
two	dimes
one	penny

3. Modify the procedure *putdata* so that the data is printed in the following form:

	Democrat	Republican	Independent
Johnson	253	75	24
Roberts	40	370	107
Saxon	98	150	228

4. Using the techniques discussed in this chapter, write a program for processing the results of a political poll. The program should read the responses obtained from the persons questioned. It should print the number of people questioned, the number of people with each combination of party affiliation and candidate preference, the number of people who prefer each candidate, and the number of people belonging to each party. All printout should be labeled with the names of the parties and candidates, where appropriate.

5. Generalize the program of Exercise 4 to handle an arbitrary number of parties and candidates (up to some reasonable limit for each). The program should begin by reading the number of parties, the names of the parties, the number of candidates, and the names of the candidates. It should then proceed as in Exercise 4.

Chapter 10

SEARCHING
AND SORTING

Searching and sorting are two operations frequently carried out on arrays. *Searching* is finding the position of a given value in an array. *Sorting* is arranging the components of an array into some desired order.

Sorting is usually done to aid later searching. For example, we would find it nearly impossible to look up a word in a dictionary or a name in a telephone directory if the entries were not in alphabetical order. Similarly, a computer can search an array much more rapidly if the components of the array are in alphabetical or numerical order.

SEARCHING

Have you ever found an item on a list by running your finger down the list until you came to the item you wanted? This kind of search is called *sequential search*. You start at the beginning of the list and examine the entries one after another until you either find the entry you are looking for or run off the end of the list.

For example, let us see how to search a one-dimensional array of integers for a given value. We declare the following variables:

list: **array**[1 . . 100] **of** *integer*;	{*list to be searched*}
size,	{*number of entries on list*}
vfind,	{*value being searched for*}
i: *integer*;	{*"finger" that keeps place in list*}
found: *Boolean*;	{*indicates whether or not the value being sought was actually found*}

The components *list*[1] through *list*[*size*] hold the list to be searched; *list*[*size*+1] through *list*[100] are currently unused but allow for future expansion of the list. We require that there be at least one unused component, which we will put to temporary use during the search.

We start with the value of i equal to 1, so that it designates the first position on the list. We then examine the entries on the list one after another. If a particular entry is the value we are seeking, then we stop the search. Otherwise, we go on to the next entry:

$i := 1;$
while $list[i] <> vfind$ **do**
$\qquad i := i+1$

If the value we are searching for is on the list, then the repetition will stop with the value of i equal to the index of the value sought. That is, when the repetition stops, the Boolean expression

$list[i] = vfind$

will be true.

Unfortunately, if the value we are looking for is not on the list, the statements just given will not work. When the value of i exceeds the value of *size*, the search continues into the unused part of the array. The program may find a spurious value equal to *vfind* on the unused part of *list*. If not, it eventually will try to refer to $list[101]$, which does not exist, and the Pascal machine will stop the program and signal an error.

In short, we need some way to keep the program from running off the end of the list if it does not find the value being sought. One way to do this is as follows. Before beginning the search, store the value of *vfind* in the first unused component, $list[size+1]$:

$list[size+1] := vfind$

This component acts as a sentinel. If the search reaches $list[size+1]$, then it finds the value being sought, and so the repetition stops.

After the repetition stops, we have to determine whether the value found was on the part of *list* currently in use, or whether the search was stopped by the sentinel. We can do this by evaluating the Boolean expression

$i <= size$

If the value of the expression is *true*, then the value found was on the part of *list* currently in use. If the value of the expression is *false*, the value being sought was not on the part of *list* currently in use, and the search was stopped by the sentinel.

The following statements search *list* for the value *vfind*. If the search is successful, then when it is over the value of *found* is *true* and the value of i is the index of the value that was found. If the search was not successful, the value of *found* is *false* and the value of *i* (which happens to be equal to *size*+1) has no significance:

```
i := 1;
list[size+1] := vfind;
while list[i] <> vfind do
    i := i+1;
found := (i <= size)
```

(Note the use of the Boolean expression $i <= size$ on the right-hand side of the assignment operator. The parentheses are not necessary, but they make the statement easier to read.)

Now let us write a program to illustrate sequential search. Our program will look up prices on a price list that has the following form:

itemnumber	price
11325	32.75
23452	12.99
37245	15.49
59217	5.64
87401	125.43
(*sentinel*)	

The arrays *itemnumber* and *price* are parallel arrays, just as we used in the last chapter. If *itemnumber*[*i*] is the number of a particular item, then *price*[*i*] (for the same value of *i*) is its price. To find the price of an item given its number, we use sequential search to find the value of *i* such that *itemnumber*[*i*] is the number of the item in question. Then *price*[*i*] is the price sought.

The program begins by reading the price list. The first line of input is the number of entries in the price list. The price list follows, each line containing an item number and a price. For the price list just given, the data is

```
5
11325       32.75
23452       12.99
37245       15.49
59217        5.64
87401      125.43
```

After the price list has been read, the program reads item numbers and prints the price of each item:

```
program prices(input, output);
var
    itemnumber: array[1 . . 101] of integer;
    price: array[1 . . 100] of real;
    size, item, i: integer;
    cost: real;
begin
    readln(size);
    for i := 1 to size do
        readln(itemnumber[i], price[i]);
    while not eof(input) do
        begin
            readln(item);
            itemnumber[size+1] := item;
            i := 1;
            while itemnumber[i] <> item do
                i := i+1;
            if i <= size then
                writeln('Price of item ', item:5, ' is ', price[i]:7:2)
            else
                writeln('Item ', item:5, ' not listed')
        end
end.
```

This program will only work for price lists having 100 or fewer entries. Why?

Binary Search

Sequential search is suitable only for short lists. For long ones it is hopelessly inefficient. For example, imagine trying to find a name in the telephone directory by starting on the first page and looking at every name until you come to the one you want.

If the names in a telephone directory were all jumbled up in some arbitrary order, then sequential search would be our only alternative. But the names are not jumbled up; they are in alphabetical order, and we use this fact to locate quickly the name we want.

One of the most efficient methods of searching an ordered list is *binary search*. Let us illustrate binary search by seeing how we might use it to find a name in the telephone directory. We start by opening the directory to the middle. This divides the directory into two parts, which we will call the left-hand part and the right-hand part. Now we look at the first name on the first page of the right-hand part. If the name we are looking for precedes this name in alphabetical order, then the name we are looking for is to be found in the left-hand part. If the name we are looking for follows the first name on the first page of the right-hand part, then it is to be found in the right-hand part.

We can now focus our attention on the half of the directory that contains the name we want and forget about the other half. In a single step we have cut in half the number of pages that we have to search. The reason we can do this is, of course, because the names are in alphabetical order.

We continue the search in the same way, at each step dividing in half the part of the directory that remains to be searched, and then narrowing the search down to either the left half or the right half. After surprisingly few halvings, the search narrows down to the page containing the desired name. This is as far as it is practical to carry binary search with a telephone directory. But with an array we can keep going until the part that remains to be searched consists of only a single component.

When we compare the name we are trying to find with the first name on the first page of the right-hand part, we might find that the two are the same. In that case we have found the name we are looking for, and we can stop the search.

The word "binary" in "binary search" refers to "two," in this case to the two parts into which we divide the portion of the list we are searching.

When the list is an array stored in computer memory, binary search works like this. We use two indices, *first* and *last*, to indicate the portion of the list that remains to be searched. At the beginning of the search *first* is given the value 1 and *last* is given the value of *size*. At any time the components that remain to be searched are

list[*first*] through *list*[*last*]

We start by examining the middle element of the part of the list that remains to be searched. The index of the middle element is:

mid := (*first* + *last*) **div** 2

Now we compare *list*[*mid*] with *vfind*. If the two values are equal then our search is over. If

vfind < *list*[*mid*]

is *true*, then *vfind* must lie in the part of the list

list[*first*] through *list*[*mid* − 1]

Therefore, we set the value of *last* to *mid* − 1

last := *mid* − 1

On the other hand, if

vfind > *list*[*mid*]

is *true* then *vfind* must lie in the part of the list

list[*mid* + 1] through *list*[*last*]

Therefore, we set the value of *first* to *mid*+1:

first := *mid*+1

One problem remains and it is the usual one: how do we stop the search if the value we are searching for is not on the list? Well, we note that at each step of the search the value of *first* is increased or the value of *last* is decreased. If the search continues fruitlessly for long enough, these two values will "pass" one another. That is,

first > *last*

When that happens, the part of the list that remains to be searched has been narrowed down to less than nothing, so we can conclude that the value we are looking for is not there.

Let us write a procedure to do a binary search. Let the array to be searched, *list*, and the number of entries on *list*, *size*, be global variables. The parameters for the procedure are *vfind*, the value being searched for, *position*, the index of *vfind* in the list, and *found*, whose value after the search indicates whether or not the value being sought was found.

```
procedure binarysearch(vfind: integer; var position: integer;
                       var found: Boolean);
var
    mid: integer;
begin
    first := 1;
    last := size;
    repeat
        mid := (first+last) div 2;
        if vfind < list[mid] then
            last := mid-1;
        if vfind > list[mid] then
            first := mid+1;
    until (vfind = list[mid]) or (first > last);
    if first <= last then
        begin
            found := true;
            position := mid
        end
    else
        found := false
end
```

For very large lists the difference between sequential search and binary search is spectacular. Suppose we have a list with one million entries. For sequential search we will have to look at 500,000 entries, on the average, before we find the right one. And the figure 500,000 *is* just an average: some searches can get by with looking at a fewer number of entries; others will have to look at many more. For instance, if the item we are looking for is the last item on the list, then we must look at one million entries to find it. And if the item being sought is not on the list, then we have to look at all one million entries to find this out. On the other hand, for a binary search of a million-entry list, we never have to look at more than 20 entries.

Searching an Index

A list or table used to help locate items in another list or table is called an *index*. Unfortunately, this meaning of the word "index" is different from the one we have employed so far in this and the previous chapter. For this section only, the word "index" will mean a table used to aid searching instead of a value used to specify a component of an array.

In everyday life we frequently use indexes to speed up searches. For example, a dictionary comes equipped with two indexes, though you may not have previously thought of them as such. One of these is the *thumb* index, which allows us to open the dictionary to the part containing words that begin with a particular letter of the alphabet. The other index consists of the *guide words* at the top of each page.

Let us focus our attention on the guide words, since they are similar to the indexes used in computer science. The guide words for each page are the first and last words on that page. By looking at the guide words we can quickly tell whether the page contains the word for which we are looking. For example, the word "computer" will not be found on the page whose guide words are "complete" and "comprehensible" but will be found on the page whose guide words are "comprehension" and "concentrate."

Now let us consider a list that is divided up into pages like a dictionary. The following declarations show the structure of this list:

type
    page = **array**[1 . . 25] **of** *integer*;
var
    indexedlist: **array**[1 . . 25] **of** *page*;
    index: **array**[1 . . 26] **of** *integer*

Figure 10–1 illustrates the structure of the arrays we have declared. *Indexedlist* is made up of 25 pages, each of which consists of 25 integers.

Now let us look at the index itself. Its entries correspond to the dictionary's guide words.

For convenience, let us suppose that only five pages of *indexedlist* are currently being used. The corresponding five entries *might* look like this:

10113–21005
22310–32541
33452–40232
45112–63451
75643–82743

These pairs of integers serve like the guide words on the dictionary pages. Thus the entry 10113–21005 tells us that the first integer on page 1 is 10113 and the last one is 21005. The entry 22310–32541 tells us that the first integer on page 2 is 22310 and the last one is 32541; and so on.

However, we can simplify this index. We do not need to know both the first and the last value stored on each page. Knowing the last value alone will be sufficient.

Suppose we write the index using the last value on each page, like this:

21005
32541
40232
63451
82743

From this index we can see that any value less than or equal to 21005, if it is in *indexedlist* at all, occurs on page 1. Any value greater than 21005 but less than or equal to 32541, if it is in *indexedlist* at all, occurs on page 2. And so on. We do not need the first value on each page to tell which page a value must be on.

Therefore, the array *index* consists of the last value on each of the pages in *indexedlist*. A variable *indexsize* has as its value the number of entries in *index*. This value is also the number of pages being used in *indexedlist*, since there is one entry in *index* for each page in *indexedlist*.

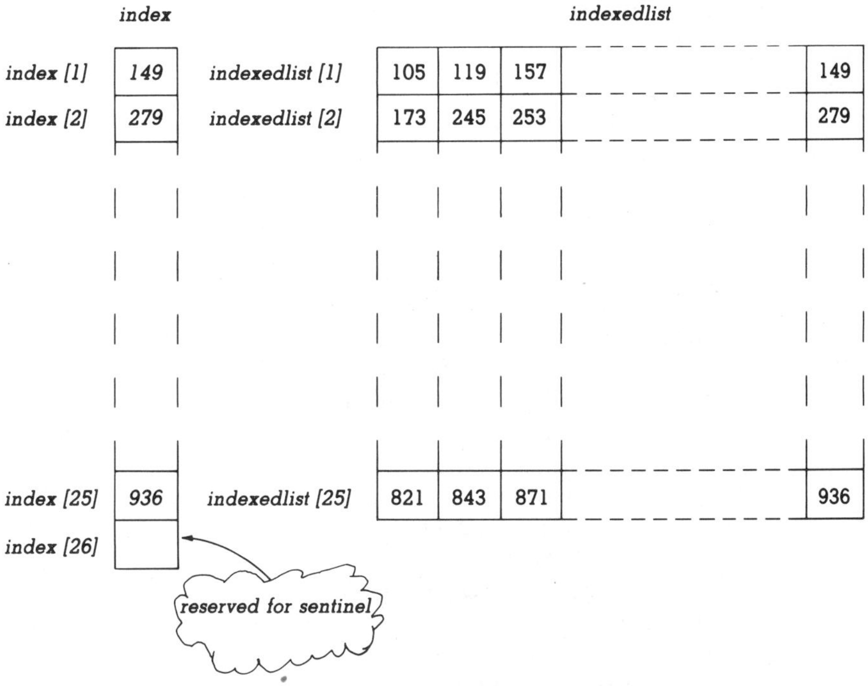

FIGURE 10-1. The array *indexedlist* is made up of 25 pages, and each page consists of 25 integers. The array *index* has 26 entries. Each of the first 25 entries is the last integer on the corresponding page of *indexedlist*. The final position of *index* is used to store a sentinel.

We can search *index* sequentially in much the same way that we search a list sequentially for a specific value. The only difference is that when we are searching an index, we stop the search not when the value we are looking for is *equal* to a particular index entry, but when it is *less than or equal* to the index entry. If the value of *vfind* is the value we are trying to look up, we can search the index as follows:

```
i := 1;
index[indexsize+1] := vfind;
while vfind > index[i] do
    i := i+1
```

As before, we use the value being searched for as a sentinel to make sure the search does not run off the end of the index. When the repetition terminates, we can check the value of *i*. If

$$i <= indexsize$$

is *true* then the page containing *vfind* (if that value is in *indexedlist* at all) is *indexedlist*[*i*]. If the value of the expression is *false*, then the value of *vfind* is greater than the largest value stored on the last page of *indexedlist*.

The search of the index, then, yields the value of the subscript *i*, which selects the page that may contain the value being searched for. The page *indexedlist*[*i*] can be searched in any desired manner to see whether or not it really contains the value of *vfind*.

SORTING

If we are to use some form of searching that is more efficient than sequential searching, then the items on the list being searched must be in some specified order. It is this order that lets us quickly find the desired item.

Therefore, computers are often called upon to arrange values in order, not only so that searching routines can do their work more efficiently, but so that humans can better find their way around in computer printout.

There are two kinds of sorting: *internal* sorting and *external* sorting. Internal sorting is used when the values to be sorted are stored in arrays in main memory. External sorting is used when the values are stored in files in auxiliary memory.

For internal sorting we assume that any one of the values to be sorted can be accessed as quickly as any other. For instance, if *a* is a 1000-component array, then we assume that the same amount of time is required to access *a*[1], *a*[500], *a*[1000], or any other component of *a*. Internal sorting routines make use of this fact in that they frequently "jump around" in the array—for instance, *a*[1], *a*[500] and *a*[1000] may all be accessed in rapid succession.

But when the values are stored in auxiliary memory, the time required to access the value in one location depends on which location was accessed last. After location 1 has been accessed, it is likely to be much quicker to access location 2 than location 500 or location 1000. This is true even for so-called random access devices such as disks. For this reason, internal sorting routines, when they will work at all with auxiliary memory devices, do so very inefficiently.

In this chapter we will confine ourselves to internal sorting routines. We will look at three sorting routines: *Bubblesort*, *Shellsort*, and *Quicksort*. They will be taken up in order of increasing efficiency and complexity. Bubblesort is easy to program but not very efficient. Quicksort lives up to its name but is more complex to program. Shellsort falls between Bubblesort and Quicksort in both complexity and efficiency.

Bubblesort

To see how Bubblesort works, let us try it out on the following list of numbers:

9   8   7   6

We begin by looking at the first two numbers, 9 and 8. Since they are out of order, we exchange them. The list now looks like this:

8   9   7   6

Now we move forward one position in the list and again compare two adjacent numbers, this time 9 and 7. Since they are out of order, we exchange them. Now the list reads

8   7   9   6

We continue through the list in this way, comparing adjacent values and exchanging them if they are out of order. We will call one such pass over the list a "compare-and-exchange pass." To display a compare-and-exchange pass in a convenient way, let us use asterisks to show which values are being compared. Thus we begin with

9*   8*   7   6

to show that 9 and 8 are being compared. We exchange them and move forward one position. This situation is displayed as follows:

8   9*   7*   6

The values 9 and 8 have been exchanged, and now we are comparing 9 and 7. With the help of this notation it is easy to show a complete compare-and-exchange pass:

9*   8*   7   6
8   9*   7*   6
8   7   9*   6*
8   7   6   9

Notice how the 9 moved all the way to the right. In a compare-and-exchange pass, the largest value that is out of order always moves as far to the right as possible. We say that it "bubbles" to the right, like a bubble rising in a container of liquid. This is the reason for the name "Bubblesort."

The list is not yet in order, although its order has been improved. We can improve the order still further by carrying out additional compare-and-exchange passes:

```
8*    7*    6     9
7     8*    6*    9
7     6     8*    9*
7     6     8     9
```

Now it is 8's turn to bubble up to its proper position. Notice that the last comparison did not produce an exchange, since the values being compared (8 and 9) were already in order.

The order of the list is now much improved, but it is not yet perfect. We still need another compare-and-exchange pass:

```
7*    6*    8     9
6     7*    8*    9
6     7     8*    9*
6     7     8     9
```

Now the 7 has bubbled into position and the list is sorted.

But how can the program tell that the list is sorted? Suppose we make another compare-and-exchange pass:

```
6*    7*    8     9
6     7*    8*    9
6     7     8*    9*
6     7     8     9
```

No exchanges are made, since all the values are in order. If any of the values were out of order, then somewhere we would have adjacent values out of order and at least one exchange would be made. Therefore, the program knows that the list is sorted when it can get through a compare-and-exchange pass without making any exchanges.

Let us use a Boolean variable *noexchanges* to indicate whether or not any exchanges have been made on a particular compare-and-exchange pass. When the pass is complete, if *noexchanges* is true then no exchanges were made during the pass.

We outline the *Bubblesort* routine as follows:

repeat
    do one compare-and-exchange pass
until *noexchanges*

A compare-and-exchange pass goes through the list comparing adjacent values and exchanging them if they are out of order. The number of values on the list is *size*. Before each pass begins, *noexchanges* is set to *true*. When an exchange is made, then *noexchanges* is set to *false*. If no exchanges are made, then *noexchanges* will retain its initial value of *true* throughout the pass. Otherwise, it will get set to *false*:

```
noexchanges := true;
for i := 1 to size−1 do
    if list[i] > list[ i+1] then
        exchange values of list[ i] and list[i+1]
        and set noexchanges to false
```

To exchange the values of two variables, we always need a third variable to hold one of the values temporarily. Let the integer variable *temporary* serve this purpose. When two adjacent values are found to be out of order, the following statements are executed:

```
temporary := list[i];
list[i] := list[i +1];
list[i+1] := temporary;
noexchanges := false
```

Putting all this together gives us the procedure *Bubblesort*. We assume that *list* and *size* are global variables.

```
procedure Bubblesort;
var
    i, temporary: integer;
    noexchanges: Boolean;
begin
    repeat
        noexchanges := true;
        for i := 1 to size−1 do
            if list[i] > list[i+1] then
                begin
                    temporary := list[i];
                    list[i] := list[i+1];
                    list[i+1] := temporary;
                    noexchanges := false
                end
    until noexchanges
end
```

We can approach the organization of a Bubblesort routine in another way. Let us go back to our example list

9   8   7   6

After the first compare-and-exchange pass, the largest value, 9, has moved into the last position:

8   7   6   9

Therefore, we can forget the last value and concentrate on the first three values. A compare-and-exchange pass over just the first three values gives us

7   6   8

Again, the largest value in the list has bubbled to the last position. Therefore, we can concentrate on the list with only two values

7   6

A compare-and-exchange pass bubbles 7 into the final position giving

6   7

and we are done.

Therefore, we are assured of sorting the entire list if we do a compare-and-exchange pass over

list[1] through *list*[*size*]

then another over

list[1] through *list*[*size*−1]

then another over

list[1] through *list*[*size*−2]

and so on until the final pass is over the

list[1], *list*[2]

We can outline this version of *Bubblesort* as follows:

for *limit* := *size* **downto** 2 **do**
    do a compare-and-exchange pass over the portion of list from *list*[1]
    through *list*[*limit*]

The compare-and-exchange pass has the same form except that *limit* is used in place of *size* and the flag *noexchanges* is no longer needed:

```
for i := 1 to limit−1 do
    if list[i] > list[i+1] then
        begin
            temporary := list[i];
            list[i] := list[i+1];
            list[i+1] := temporary
        end
```

Putting the parts together gives us the procedure *Bubblesrt*.

```
procedure Bubblesrt;
var
    i, temporary, limit: integer;
begin
    for limit := size downto 2 do
        for i := 1 to limit−1 do            IF list[i] > list[i+1] THEN
            begin
                temporary := list[i];
                list[i] := list[i+1];
                list[i+1] := temporary
            end
end
```

THE ONE THAT WORKS

Which version of Bubblesort is the best? *Bubblesrt* always does *size*−1 compare-and-exchange passes, even if the first pass happened to put the list in order. The original *Bubblesort* will stop as soon as it can make a pass without having to do any exchanges.

This argument seems to favor *Bubblesort*; however, we can raise this question: For an arbitrary list, how likely is it that *Bubblesort* will be able to stop before doing *size*−1 passes? This turns out not to be very likely. Unless we know in advance that none of the values are very far from their final positions, the chances are that *Bubblesort* will have to run for close to *size*−1 passes.

Given that both versions will probably make about the same number of compare-and-exchange passes, which version is more efficient? *Bubblesort* requires that we keep track of a Boolean variable *noexchanges* which must be set to *true* at the beginning of each pass, set to *false* after each exchange, and tested after each pass. *Bubblesrt* controls the number of passes with a **for** statement. Most Pascal machines can execute the **for** statement more efficiently than they can manipulate the Boolean variable, so *Bubblesrt* will often execute faster than *Bubblesort* (although the difference may be quite marginal). Also, *Bubblesrt* saves some time in that, after the first pass, each succeeding pass is over only a part of the list, a part whose size decreases with each pass.

Manipulations that are necessary to control the operation of a program are known as *overhead* or *bookkeeping*. For small lists—10 or 11 components, say—*Bubblesort* will often outperform the other more sophisticated routines we are going to discuss because *Bubblesort* does less bookkeeping than the other routines. But when the lists become longer, the extra bookkeeping pays for itself, and the other routines become more efficient.

Shellsort

A problem with Bubblesort is that while values move toward their proper positions rapidly in one direction, they move slowly in the other. Again going back to our example,

9   8   7   6

after one compare-and-exchange pass we have

8   7   6   9

The value 9 has moved rapidly all the way in to the end of the list. However, 6 has only moved one position in the direction of its final position. We see that the largest value moves rapidly to its final position. But other values move much more slowly, often only one position per pass.

Shellsort (it is named after its inventor, Donald Shell) improves matters as follows. A series of compare-and-exchange passes are made, but adjacent items are not compared. Instead there is a fixed gap between the items that are compared and exchanged. When no more exchanges can be made for a given gap, the gap is narrowed, and the compare-and-exchange passes continue. The final passes are made with a gap of 1, just as in *Bubblesort*.

What happens is that the earlier passes quickly move values that are far out of position closer to their final positions. Thus the later passes with narrower gaps have much less work to do.

For example, let us take the example list we have used all along and make a pass with a gap of 2. That is, we compare $list[1]$ with $list[3]$ and $list[2]$ with $list[4]$:

9*   8   7*   6
7   8*   9   6*
7   6   9   8

Notice how far 6 has moved toward its final position. A second compare-and-exchange pass with a gap of 2 makes no exchanges:

7*   6   9*   8
7   6*   9   8*
7   6   9   8

Since we can make no more exchanges with a gap of 2, we divide the gap in half and continue with a gap of 1:

7*   6*   9   8
6   7*   9*   8
6   7   9*   8*
6   7   8   9

The list is now in order but the program will take another pass to find this out. Since it can make a pass with a gap of 1 without making any exchanges, the list is sorted and *Shellsort* can terminate.

Actually, if you compare the sorting of this example with that done by *Bubblesort*, you will see that *Shellsort* required just as many passes. It is only for lists larger than 10 or 11 values that *Shellsort* can be expected to be more efficient than *Bubblesort*.

We start off with a gap equal to one-half the size of the list. Each time we need a new gap, we divide the old gap in half (ignoring any remainder). The final gap used is always 1. Actually, better methods of choosing the series of gaps are known, but they are more difficult to program than the method just given. Since the given method is not bad and is easy to program, it is often used.

We can outline *Shellsort* as follows:

```
gap := size div 2;
repeat
    do a "bubblesort" but comparing and exchanging
    list [i] and list[i+gap] instead of list[i] and
    list [i+1]
    gap := gap div 2
until gap < 1
```

Modifying the *Bubblesort* routine as indicated and adding the extra level of repetition gives us *Shellsort*:

```
procedure Shellsort;
var
    i, temporary, gap: integer;
    noexchanges: Boolean;
begin
    gap := size div 2;
    repeat
      repeat
          noexchanges := true;
          for i := 1 to size−gap do
            if list[i] > list[i+gap] then
                begin
                    temporary := list[i];
                    list[i] := list[i+gap];
                    list[i+gap] := temporary;
                    noexchanges := false
                end
      until noexchanges;
        gap := gap div 2
    until gap < 1
end
```

Notice that in the "Bubblesort" part of the program, *gap* plays the role that was taken by 1 in the original *Bubblesort*.

Shellsort is a good, general purpose sorting routine that can be used satisfactorily with lists having a couple of hundred values.

Quicksort

When lists are very long or speed is of the essence, we can use a routine called *Quicksort* that is faster than *Shellsort*. In fact, *Quicksort* is one of the fastest internal sorting routines known. As you might expect, it is more complicated than either *Bubblesort* or *Shellsort*.

We begin by considering a list of numbers to be sorted:

3 9 6 5 7 4 1 2 8

We want to divide this list into two sublists in such a way that all the values on the first sublist are less than all the values on the second sublist. To do this, we choose one of the numbers to serve as a dividing line between the two sublists. All the numbers less than the dividing-line value go on the first sublist; all those greater than the dividing-line value go on the second sublist. The dividing-line value itself can end up on either sublist.

For example, let us choose the dividing-line value to be 7, the value at the midpoint of the original list. Then we can divide the list into sublists as follows:

3 2 6 5 1 4   7 9 8

All the values less than 7 are on the first sublist, and all the values greater than 7 are on the second, as is 7 itself. Furthermore, if we take the two sublists together as making one large list, a measure of order has been introduced in the large list, since all the values less than 7 have been moved to the left and all the values greater than 7 have been moved to the right.

Quicksort continues by carrying out on the sublists the same process that was carried out on the original list. Let us see how repeatedly carrying out this process on smaller and smaller sublists will eventually result in the original list being sorted.

Let us start with the second sublist

7 9 8

We take the middle value, 9, as the dividing line. The list can be divided as follows:

7 8   9

Since the "list" 9 consists of a single value, it can be divided no further. The list

7 8

can be divided in only one way

7   8

Now let us see how the original list has been divided so far:

3 2 6 5 1 4   7   8   9

We see that what was the second sublist of the original division has been completely sorted by applying to it the same process that was applied to the original list.

Now let us apply the same process to the first sublist of the original division:

3 2 6 5 1 4

If we take 6 as the dividing-line value, we get the division

3 2 4 5 1   6

The second of these cannot be further divided. Using 4 as the dividing-line value, the first can be divided as follows:

3 2 1   5 4

Of these two sublists, the second can only be divided into

4   5

and the first can be divided into

1   2   3

(*Quicksort* occasionally divides a list into three sublists. The middle sublist always consists of the dividing-line value alone.)

Now let us see how these repeated divisions into sublists have put the original list in order:

```
3 9 6 5 7 4 1 2 8
3 2 6 5 1 4      7 9 8
3 2 6 5 1 4      7 8        9
3 2 6 5 1 4      7        8        9
3 2 4 5 1      6        7        8        9
3 2 1      5 4      6        7        8        9
3 2 1      4      5      6      7      8        9
1      2      3      4      5      6      7      8      9
```

Let us look at the things we have to do to bring about this division of the original list into successively small sublists:

1. We have to choose the value that will serve as the dividing-line value.

2. We have to rearrange the values on the original list so that all those values less than the dividing-line value are to the left of a certain point and all those greater than the dividing-line value are to the right of the same point.

3. We have to repeat the same process for the two sublists we have created. This can be done by using *recursion*. That is, we call the procedure *Quicksort*, the one that we are writing, to sort the sublists. When the two sublists have been sorted, then the original list also will be sorted.

Our first job is to find the dividing-line value. *Quicksort* works most efficiently when the two sublists are nearly the same size. They will be nearly the same size if the dividing-line value is the *median* of the values on the original list: the value such that there are as many values less than or equal to it as there are greater than or equal to it. The median of the list we used as an example is 5.

Unfortunately, finding the median of a list of values is almost as hard as sorting the values, so using the median is not practical. We must choose one of the values and hope that it is close to the median. If the values are in random order, then any choice is as good as any other, since any value is as likely as any other to be close to the median.

However, there is an argument for taking a value near the middle of the list. Often we are called upon to sort a list that is almost in order—only a small number of values are out of order. In fact, a list that is supposed to be in order may be sorted for good measure. In these cases a value near the center of the list has a good chance of being close to the median. Therefore this is the choice we will make for the dividing-line value.

Thus for the list

```
3  9  6  5  7  4  1  2  8
```

we chose the middle value 7 for the dividing-line value, and this was not too bad a choice, since 7 is not too far from the median, 5. On the other hand, for the sublist

```
3  2  6  5  1  4
```

we chose 6, a terrible choice. Since 6 is the largest value on the list, using it produces the very unequal division

```
3  2  4  5  1      6
```

It turns out that, on the average, the terrible choices are few enough so that they do not seriously affect the efficiency of the routine.

The next step is to rearrange the values so as to produce the two sublists. We start with two arrows, one at each end of the list:

```
3 9 6 5 7 4 1 2 8
↑               ↑
i               j
```

The two arrows are labeled *i* and *j*, since *i* and *j* are the array indices that will be used to represent the arrows in the program.

The arrow *i* is moved forward through the list as long as it points to a value less than the dividing-line value. When it reaches a value greater than or equal to the dividing-line value, it stops. The arrow *j* moves backward through the list as long as it points to a value greater than the dividing-line value. When it reaches a value less than or equal to the dividing-line value, it stops.

Remembering that the dividing-line value is 7, moving arrow *i* gives us

```
3 9 6 5 7 4 1 2 8
  ↑           ↑
  i           j
```

and moving arrow *j* gives us

```
3 9 6 5 7 4 1 2 8
  ↑         ↑
  i         j
```

The values pointed to by *i* and *j* are exchanged

```
3 2 6 5 7 4 1 9 8
  ↑         ↑
  i         j
```

after which *i* is moved forward one position and *j* is moved backward one position:

```
3 2 6 5 7 4 1 9 8
    ↑     ↑
    i     j
```

Now the process is repeated: *i* is moved forward until it encounters a value too large for the first sublist and *j* is moved backward until it encounters a value too small for the second sublist:

```
3 2 6 5 7 4 1 9 8
      ↑ ↑
      i j
```

(Notice that j does not have to move since it is already pointing to a value too small for the second sublist.) Again we exchange the values

```
3 2 6 5 1 4 7 9 8
      ↑   ↑
      i   j
```

and move both i forward one place and j backward one place:

```
3 2 6 5 1 4 7 9 8
        ↑
        i, j
```

Again we move i forward and j backward in search of out-of-place values:

```
3 2 6 5 1 4 7 9 8
      ↑ ↑
      j i
```

But at this point the two arrows have passed each other, and this signals that our job is done. Everything from the beginning of the list through the value pointed to by j constitutes the first sublist and everything from the value pointed to by i through the end of the list constitutes the second sublist. Thus we divide as follows:

```
3 2 6 5 1 4   7 9 8
      ↑   ↑
      j   i
```

Finally, the same procedure has to be applied to each of the two sublists. We do this with recursive calls to the procedure *Quicksort*.

Now let us outline the procedure. The formal parameters of *Quicksort* will be *first* and *last*, the indices of the first and last values on the list or sublist to be sorted:

```
procedure Quicksort(first, last: integer);
var
    i, j, dividingline: integer;
begin
    i := first;
    j := last;
    dividingline := list[(first+last) div 2];
    repeat
        move i forward as long as list[i] is less than dividingline
        move j backward as long as list[j] is greater than dividingline
        if i <= j then
            exchange values of list[i] and list[j]; move i forward one place and
            j backward one place
```

until $i > j$;
if *first* is less than j then call *Quicksort* to sort the sublist *list*[*first*]
through *list*[*j*]; if i is less than *last* then call *Quicksort* to sort the sublist
list[*i*] through *list*[*last*]
end

With this outline, we have no trouble writing the actual procedure:

```
procedure Quicksort(first, last: integer);
var
    i, j, dividingline, temporary: integer;
begin
    i := first;
    j := last;
    dividingline := list[(first + last) div 2];
    repeat
        while list[i] < dividingline do
            i := i+1;
        while list[j] > dividingline do
            j := j-1;
        if i <= j then
            begin
                temporary := list[i];
                list[i] := list[j];
                list[j] := temporary;
                i := i+1;
                j := j-1
            end
    until i > j;
    if first < j then Quicksort(first, j);
    if i < last then Quicksort(i, last)
end
```

This version of *Quicksort* contains two recursive calls to *Quicksort* itself. On some computer systems recursion is inefficient and in some programming languages it is not permitted at all. Therefore, we will improve the usefulness of *Quicksort* if we can reduce the amount of recursion or eliminate it altogether. We will see that it is easy to eliminate one of the recursive calls to *Quicksort* but eliminating the other one takes more work.

When a recursive call occurs at the end of a procedure, we can always eliminate it by repeating the body of the procedure instead of calling the procedure recursively. In particular, we can replace

everything up to the last line of *Quicksort*
if $i <$ *last* **then** *Quicksort*(*i*, *last*)

by

```
repeat
     everything up to the last line of Quicksort
     first := i
until first >= last
```

That is, instead of calling *Quicksort* with *i* as the actual parameter corresponding to the formal parameter *first*, we just set *first* to the value of *i* and repeat the statements of *Quicksort*. The condition *first* >= *last* in the **repeat** statement serves the same purpose as the condition *i* < *last* in the **if** statement of the original version. Both make sure that the program does not attempt to sort a sublist that consists of only one value.

The procedure *Quicksrt*, which incorporates this idea, contains only one recursive call:

```
procedure Quicksrt(first, last: integer);
var
     i, j, dividingline, temporary: integer;
begin
   i := first
   repeat
       j := last;
       dividingline := list[(first+last) div 2];
       repeat
           while list[i] < dividingline do
               i := i+1;
           while list[j] > dividingline do
               j := j-1;
           if i <= j then
               begin
                   temporary := list[i];
                   list[i] := list[j];
                   list[j] := temporary;
                   i := i+1;
                   j := j-1
               end
       until i > j;
       if first < j then Quicksrt(first, j);
       first := i
   until first >= last
end
```

The statement

```
i := first
```

was moved out of the repetition since at the end of each repetition the values of *i* and *first* are equal. Therefore, this statement needs to be executed only once, at the beginning of the procedure.

Eliminating the remaining recursion takes more work. The problem is this. At the point where the recursive call to *Quicksort* is made, the values of *first* and *j* are the limits of a sublist that needs to be sorted. If we go on with the procedure being executed and do not make the recursive call, then the values of *first* and *j* will be changed. Therefore, the values of *first* and *j* have to be saved so that we can come back and search the corresponding sublist later.

We can save the values of *first* and *j* using a data structure known as a *stack*. The stack consists of a list of values together with the index of the last value on the list. The position of the last value is the top of the stack. As with an ordinary stack such as a stack of papers or cards, new values are placed on the top of the stack or removed from the top of the stack.

We can declare the stack and the index that gives the position of its top as follows:

stack: **array**[1..50] **of** *integer*;
top: 1..50;

We can visualize a stack that contains four values like this:

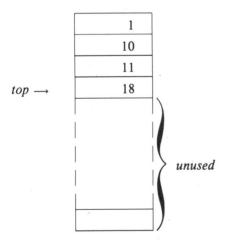

Notice that the top of the stack is actually on the "bottom" when the array is diagramed in the normal fashion. In our discussion we will use an abbreviated form of this diagram:

```
           1
          10
          11
top  →    18
```

Suppose we want to put a new value on top of the stack. First we move *top* forward one place so that it points to an unused position:

$top := top + 1$

This gives us

```
        1
       10
       11
       18
top →
```

Now we assign the value we want to put on the stack to *stack*[*top*]:

$stack[top] := 19$

The stack now looks like this:

```
         1
        10
        11
        18
top →   19
```

To remove a value from the top of the stack, we first assign the value of *stack*[*top*] to the variable that is to receive the value

$i := stack[top]$

The value assigned to *i* is 19. Now we move *top* back one position so that it points to the current top value:

$top := top - 1$

Now the stack looks like this:

```
         1
        10
        11
top →   18
```

We will use the stack to hold the indices delimiting sublists that have yet to be sorted. Thus at the beginning of the procedure, 1 and *size*, which delimit the entire list, are placed on the stack:

$stack[1] := 1;$
$stack[2] := size;$
$top := 2$

At the point in *Quicksrt* where *Quicksrt* is called recursively to sort a sublist

if *first* $<$ *j* **then** *Quicksrt*(*first*, *j*)

we now place the values of *first* and *j* on the stack so that the procedure will come back and sort this sublist later:

```
if first < j then
    begin
        top := top+1;
        stack[top] := first;
        top := top+1;
        stack[top] := j
    end
```

We can outline the nonrecursive version of *Quicksort* as follows:

```
procedure Quiksort;
var
    i, j, dividingline, temporary,
    first, last: integer;
begin
    stack[1] := 1;
    stack[2] := size;
    top := 2;
    repeat
        last := stack[top];
        top := top-1;
        first := stack[top];
        top := top-1;
        i := first;
        repeat
            j := last;
            dividingline := list[(first+last) div 2]
            divide the list list[first] through list[last] into sublists list[first]
            through list[j] and list[i] through list[last]
            if first < j then
                begin
                    top := top+1;
                    stack[top] := first;
                    top := top+1;
                    stack[top] := j
                end;
            first := i
        until first >= last
    until top = 0
end
```

As you see, the outermost repetition

repeat

  .

  .

  .

until *top* = 0

removes a pair of indices from the stack and processes the corresponding sublist. This is repeated until the stack is empty—that is, until *top* = 0.

   Each sublist is processed by dividing it into two parts as usual. The indices for the left part are put on the stack. The right part is again subdivided. The repetition

repeat

  .

  .

  .

until *first* >= *last*

repeats the subdivision process until a right part consisting of a single value is obtained. When this repetition terminates, two new indices are obtained from the stack and the subdivision process is repeated once again. Here is the complete procedure:

```
procedure Quicksort;
var
    i, j, dividingline, temporary,
    first, last: integer;
begin
    stack[1] := 1;
    stack[2] := size;
    top := 2;
    repeat
        last := stack[top];
        top := top−1;
        first:= stack[top];
        top := top−1;
        i := first;
        repeat
            j := last;
            dividingline := list[(first+last) div 2];
            repeat
                while list[i] < dividingline do
                    i := i+1;
                while list[j] > dividingline do
                    j := j−1;
```

```
                          if i <= j then
                              begin
                                  temporary := list[i];
                                  list[i] := list[j];
                                  list[j] := temporary;
                                  i := i+1;
                                  j := j−1
                              end
                      until i > j;
                      if first < j then
                          begin
                              top := top+1;
                              stack[top] := first;
                              top := top+1;
                              stack[top] := j
                          end;
                      first := i
                  until first >= last
              until top = 0
end
```

This example illustrates another way to use recursion—as a step in designing a program. Our first recursive version of *Quicksort* was straightforward to construct and to understand. The final nonrecursive version is much more complex, and would be quite hard to construct and understand from scratch. But by starting with the recursive version and then modifying it to remove the recursion we did not have too much trouble arriving at the more complicated nonrecursive version. To put it another way, recursion is a useful way of *thinking* about programming even if the actual function or procedure that we finally arrive at turns out to be nonrecursive.

EXERCISES

1. We want to store a small telephone directory in the computer and let the computer look up numbers for us. The directory has the following form:

Bill   651–4837
Frank   572–4351
Jane   613–3427
Mary   547–9081
Sue   553–7980

Both the names and the phone numbers should be stored as packed arrays of characters. Write a program to read in the directory, then read names and print the corresponding phone numbers. The program should use sequential search.

2. The same as Exercise 1 except that the program should use binary search. What condition must the directory satisfy in order for binary search to be used?

3. Modify the program of Exercise 2 so that it will read a directory in which the names are in arbitrary order and sort the names into alphabetical order. The program should use *Bubblesort* (either version). Remember that when two names are exchanged, the corresponding phone numbers have to be exchanged as well!

4. The same as Exercise 3 except use *Shellsort*.

5. The same as Exercise 3 except use *Quicksort* (any version).

6. When the size of the sublist being sorted becomes less than ten values, Quicksort becomes inefficient because of the overhead associated with calling recursive subroutines or manipulating the stack. For short lists, a low-overhead sorting method such as *Bubblesort* will do a better job. Therefore, let us modify the *Quicksort* routines as follows: (a) The *Quicksort* routine will not attempt to sort sublists of ten values or less—these will be treated as the present routines treat sublists of one value. (b) After the *Quicksort* is finished, the sorting will be completed by making nine compare-and-exchange passes over the entire list. Why can we be sure that nine compare-and-exchange passes are sufficient?

7. Many Pascal machines allow a program to read a clock built into the computer. By reading the clock before a procedure is called and again after it returns, the program can determine the time required for the procedure to execute. If your Pascal machine has this facility, use it to time the various sorting procedures to determine their relative efficiency. The values to be sorted should be chosen at random. For instance, using the *random* function discussed in Chapter 7, the expression

trunc(10000.0*random) + 1

will generate a random integer in the range 1–10000. You should experiment with lists of different sizes as well. Of course, when comparing two routines, both should sort lists of the same size and containing the same values. (Note that by giving the seed the same starting value, *random* can be made to generate the same set of "random" numbers more than once.)

Chapter 11

STRUCTURED TYPES: RECORDS

Arrays have two outstanding characteristics: (1) All the components of an array are of the same data type. (2) The index used to refer to a particular component of an array can be computed during the execution of the program—at "execution time."

A *record* is the opposite of an array in both these respects. The components of a record (known as *fields*) can be of different data types and usually are. And the *field identifiers* by which record components are referenced cannot be computed at execution time but must be specified when the program is written.

We used words such as "list" and "table" and "book" to help us visualize arrays. For records the word "record" itself should suffice, for it brings to mind the collections of diverse information found in school records, employment records, medical records, and the like. A record in computer science is just such a collection of different types of data.

RECORD DEFINITIONS

The following example illustrates the definition of a record data type:

type
    weather = **record**
                sky: (*cloudy, ptycldy, clear*);
                precip: (*rain, snow, sleet, hail, none*);
                low,
                high: *integer*
          end;

Here *weather* is the record type being defined. The identifiers *sky*, *precip*, *low*, and *high* are the field identifiers. They are used to refer to the components of a value of type *weather*.

For instance, suppose variables *u*, *v*, and *w* are variables of type *weather*:

var
    u, *v*, *w*: *weather*;

We can think of *w*, say, as naming a memory location made up of four smaller locations, one for each component of a value of type *weather*:

w	*cloudy*
	rain
	50
	75

We can refer to particular components of the value of *w* as follows: the variable name *w* is followed by a period and the appropriate field identifier. The result is known as a *field designator* and names the location holding the corresponding component. Thus the locations making up *w* are named as follows:

w.sky	*cloudy*
w.precip	*rain*
w.low	50
w.high	75

The field designators can be used just like any other variables. For instance,

w.sky := *ptycldy*

changes the contents of *w.sky* to *ptycldy*,

writeln(*w.low*, *w.high*)

causes the computer to print

50   75

and

i := *w.high*−*w.low*

assigns to *i* the value 25.

Note that the field designator

w.sky

is similar to the indexed variable

a[3]

The record variable *w* corresponds to the array variable *a*. The period in the field designator corresponds to the brackets in the indexed variable. And the field identifer *sky* corresponds to the index 3.

But do not forget the differences: The indexed variables of an array all have the same data type. The field designations in general have different data types. The index of an indexed variable can be computed as the program executes. The field identifier of a field designator must be specified when the program is written.

As was the case for array variables, the value of one record variable can be assigned to another record variable of the same type. Thus

v := *w*

is equivalent to

v.sky := *w.sky*;
v.precip := *w.precip*;
v.low := *w.low*;
v.high := *w.high*

The following are some other typical examples of definitions of record types:

employee = **record**
              ssnumber: **packed array**[1..9] **of** *char*;
              name,
              address: **packed array**[1..40] **of** *char*;
              payrate: *real*;
              mstatus: (*single, married, divorced*);
              numdependents: *integer*
         end;

car = **record**
          make,
          model,
          bodytype,
          color: **packed array**[1..10] **of** *char*;
          weight: *integer*
        end;

```
book = record
           title: packed array[1..80] of char;
           author,
           publisher,
           city: packed array[1..20] of char;
           year: integer;
           price: real
       end;


passenger = record
               name: packed array[1..20] of char;
               flight,
               seat: packed array[1..4] of char;
               phoneno: packed array[1..10] of char
           end;


date = record
           month: (jan, feb, mar, apr, may, june,
                     july, aug, sept, oct, nov, dec);
           dayofweek: (mon, tue, wed, thurs, fri, sat, sun);
           dayofmonth: 1..31;
           year: integer
       end;


fraction = record
              numerator,
              denominator: integer
           end;
```

NESTED RECORDS

It is possible for a field of a record to itself be another record. For instance, suppose we define the record type *day* as follows:

```
day = record
         dt: date;
         wx: weather
      end;
```

A value of type *day* will have as its fields values of types *date* and *weather*. Since *date* and *weather* are themselves record types, a record of type *day* contains records of types *date* and *weather*.

For instance, suppose we declare

```
today: day;
```

Then *today.dt* and *today.wx* are variables of type *date* and *weather*, respectively. To refer to the fields of the values of *today.dt* and *today.wx*, we must append an additional field identifier:

today.dt.month
today.dt.dayofmonth
today.dt.dayofweek
today.dt.year
today.wx.sky
today.wx.precip
today.wx.low
today.wx.high

These field designators can be used to assign values to the fields of the value of *today*. For instance:

today.dt.month := *may*;
today.dt.dayofmonth := 24;
today.dt.dayofweek := *thurs*;
today.dt.year := 1979;
today.wx.sky := *cloudy*;
today.wx.precip := *rain*;
today.wx.low := 55;
today.wx.high := 75

We can think of *today* as referring to an area of memory laid out as follows:

today.dt.month	*may*
today.dt.dayofmonth	24
today.dt.dayofweek	*thurs*
today.dt.year	1979
today.wx.sky	*cloudy*
today.wx.precip	*rain*
today.wx.low	55
today.wx.high	75

It is not necessary for the nested records to be defined as separate data types. For instance, declarations like the following are permitted:

person: **record**
        name: **record**
            first,
            middle,
            last: **packed array**$[1..20]$ **of** *char*
          end;
        addr: **record**
           street,
           city: **packed array**$[1..40]$ **of** *char*;
           state: **packed array**$[1..2]$ **of** *char*;
           zip: **packed array**$[1..5]$ **of** *char*
          end
      end;

The following field designators can be used to refer to fields of the value of *person*:

person.name
person.addr
person.name.first
person.name.middle
person.name.last
person.addr.street
person.addr.city
person.addr.state
person.addr.zip

The with Statement   Writing field designators can be rather clumsy, particularly when the fields of one record are themselves records, since we have to use a long string of field identifiers to specify the field to which we want to refer.

Another problem arises when we refer to different fields of the same record. For instance, suppose the array *report* is declared as follows

report: **array**$[1..7]$ **of** *weather*;

When we refer to *report*[*i*], the computer has to do a calculation to locate in memory the record corresponding to the value of *i*. When we refer to

report[*i*].*sky*
report[*i*].*precip*
report[*i*].*low*
report[*i*].*high*

the computer will probably do the calculation for locating *report*[*i*] four times—once to refer to the *sky* field, once to refer to the *precip* field, once to refer to the *low* field, and once to refer to the *high* field. We need some way of telling the computer to locate a record once and then remember its location while we are referring to its fields.

The **with** statement allows us to refer to the fields of a record using the field identifiers alone. We can refer to a field deep within a nested set of records without having to write a long string of field identifiers. And the computer only needs to locate a record once no matter how many references we make to its fields.

For example, let us use a **with** statement to assign values to the fields of *w*:

```
with w do
    begin
        sky := cloudy;
        precip := rain;
        low := 55;
        high := 75
    end
```

This is equivalent to

```
w.sky := cloudy;
w.precip := rain;
w.low := 55;
w.high := 75
```

Putting the assignments in the **with** statement takes the place of prefixing every field identifier with

w.

We could use the same technique for *report*[*i*]:

```
with report[i] do
    begin
        sky := clear;
        precip := none;
        low := 28;
        high := 45
    end
```

The record *report*[*i*] is located once, after which all its fields are modified.

We can list more than one record variable in a **with** statement and then refer to the fields of all the record variables listed. This feature is particularly useful when dealing with nested records. For instance, consider the record variable *today* of type *day* that we talked about earlier. To refer to the fields of *today* and of *today.dt* and *today.wx*, we use the **with** statement beginning with

with *today*, *dt*, *wx* **do**

Notice that once *today* has been listed, the computer will prefix *today.* to field identifiers when necessary. Therefore we need only list *dt* and *wx* instead of *today.dt* and *today.wx*. The **with** statement allows us to refer to the fields of *today*, *today.dt*, and *today.wx* by their field identifiers. The assignments illustrated in the previous section can be made as follows:

```
with today, dt, wx do
    begin
        month := may;
        dayofmonth := 24;
        dayofweek := thurs;
        year := 1979;
        sky := cloudy;
        precip := rain;
        low := 55;
        high := 75
    end
```

RECORD VARIANTS

Sometimes we want to consider record values to be of the same data type even though they have different structures. Pascal allows a record to have a *variant part* that can have different structures for different records of the same type.

For example, a bibliography usually contains references to both books and magazine articles. But references to books have a different form than references to magazine articles. For a book the author, title, city of publication, publisher, and year of publication are given. For a magazine article, we need the author, the title of the article, the name of the magazine, the month and year of publication, and the pages on which the article begins and ends.

Since the author, title, and year of publication are the same for both books and magazine articles, they will always be present. But the city of publication and the publisher will be present only in references to books. The magazine name, the month of publication, and the beginning and ending pages will only be present in references to magazine articles.

We also need some way of distinguishing references to books from references to magazine articles, so that the computer can determine the structure of the value it is dealing with. For that purpose, let us define a type

reftype = (*book*, *magazine*)

whose values can be used to distinguish the two kinds of references.

We can define a type *reference*, which includes references to both book and magazine articles, as follows:

```
reference = record
                author: packed array[1..40] of char;
                title: packed array[1..80] of char;
                year: integer;
```

```
            case kind: reftype of
              book: (city: packed array [1..20] of char;
                      publisher: packed array [1..10] of char);
              magazine: (name: packed array[1..20] of char;
                          month: (jan, feb, mar, apr, may, jun,
                                  july, aug, sept, oct, nov, dec);
                          pages: packed array [1..7] of char)
      end;
```

The record has a *fixed part*, which is the same for every value of type *reference*, and a *variant part*, which is different for different values of type *reference*. The fixed part always comes first and the variant part afterward. Everything through

case *kind*: *reftype* **of**

belongs to the fixed part of the record. Everything following this belongs to the variant part.

Thus all values of type reference will have fields *author*, *title*, *year*, and *kind*. However some will have fields *city* and *publisher* and some will have fields *name*, *month*, and *pages*.

The field *kind*, the one that occurs between **case** and **of**, is called the *tag field*. Its value determines which structure a particular value has. Thus if the value of *kind* is *book* then the program will know it is dealing with a reference to a book; if the value of *kind* is *magazine*, then the program will know it is dealing with a reference to a magazine.

The possible values of the tag field are used to label the variant parts of the record. The two possible values of *kind* are *book* and *magazine*, and they label the variant parts as follows:

book: (variant part for a book reference);
magazine: (variant part for a magazine article reference)

Each variant part is enclosed in parentheses.

Thus, for a reference to a book, the value of *kind* is *book*, and the record has the same structure as if it has been defined as:

```
record
    author: packed array[1..40] of char;
    title: packed array[1..80] of char;
    year: integer;
    kind: reftype;
    city: packed array[1..20] of char;
    publisher: packed array[1..10] of char
end
```

For a reference to a magazine article, the value of *kind* is *magazine*, and the record has the same structure as if it had been defined as:

record
    author: **packed array**[1 . . 40] **of** *char*;
    title: **packed array**[1 . . 80] **of** *char*;
    year: *integer*;
    kind: *reftype*;
    name: **packed array**[1 . . 20] **of** *char*;
    month: (*jan, feb, mar, apr, may, jun,*
            july, aug, sept, oct, nov, dec);
    pages: **packed array**[1 . . 7] **of** *char*
end

It is not necessary for the record to contain a tag field. In that case, no part of the record specifies which possible structure it has, and the program must get that information from elsewhere. For instance, we could define the type *reference* without the tag field *kind*:

reference = **record**
                author: **packed array**[1 . . 40] **of** *char*;
                title: **packed array**[1 . . 80] **of** *char*;
                year: *integer*;
                case *reftype* **of**
                    book: (*city*: **packed array**[1 . . 20] **of** *char*;
                          publisher: **packed array**[1 . . 10] **of** *char*);
                    magazine: (*name*: **packed array**[1 . . 20] **of** *char*;
                          month: (*jan, feb, mar, apr,*
                                may, jun, july, aug,
                                sept, oct, nov, dec);
                      pages: **packed array** [1 . . 7] **of** *char*)
        end;

Now a value of type reference may consist of the fields *author, title, year, city,* and *publisher* or *author, title, year, name, month,* and *pages*. It is up to the program to know which structure a particular value has. The line

case *reftype* **of**

indicates that values of type *reftype* will be used to label the variant parts in the record definition. However, no field is declared to be of type *reftype*.

THE SCOPES OF FIELD IDENTIFIERS

The scope of a field identifier is the record in which it occurs. If the field identifier occurs in several nested records, then its scope is the smallest record in which it occurs.

This means that the same field identifier can be used in different records:

```
var
    u: record
        a,
        b: integer
    end;
    v: record
        a,
        b: real
    end;
```

There is no difficulty distinguishing the field identifiers of the different records:

```
u.a := 5;
u.b := 25;
v.a := 7.2;
v.b := 6.3
```

The integer values are assigned to the fields of the record variable *u*; the real values are assigned to the fields of the record variable *v*. The same statements could also have been written:

```
with u do
    begin
        a := 5;
        b := 25
    end;
with v do
    begin
        a := 7.2;
        b := 6.3
    end
```

It is also possible to use the same identifiers for variable names and field identifiers:

```
var
    a, b: Boolean;
    u: record
        a, b: integer
    end;
    v: record
        a, b: real
    end;
```

With these declarations the following statements are valid:

```
a := true;        b := false;
u.a := 5;         u.b := 25;
v.a := 7.2;       v.b := 6.3
```

These statements could also be written:

```
a := true;    b := false;
with u do
    begin
        a := 5;    b := 25
    end;
with v do
    begin
        a := 7.2;    b := 6.3
    end
```

Note that the field identifiers in the variant part of a record all have the same scope. Therefore, it is *not* permissible to use the same identifier in different variants. For instance, we are sometimes tempted to make incorrect declarations like the following:

```
u: record
        a: integer;
        case b: Boolean of
            true: (c: integer);
            false: (c: real)
    end;
```

The idea is to let c be an integer field when the value of b is *true* and a real field when the value of b is *false*. But this does not work, since both cs are in the same scope so their definitions conflict with one another. We must use different identifiers for the integer field and the real field:

```
u: record
        a: integer;
        case b: Boolean of
            true: (ci: integer);
            false: (cr: real)
    end;
```

This way, the Pascal machine always knows that $u.ci$ represents an integer value and $u.cr$ represents a real value. If our previous declaration had been allowed, the Pascal machine would not have been able to tell whether $u.c$ represented an integer or a real value.

It is worth repeating here what was said earlier in connection with functions and subroutines. Just because Pascal allows us to use the same name for different things does not mean that we should do so without good reason.

POINTER TYPES

The variables we have dealt with so far are said to be *static*, since they are declared when the program is written and remain in existence throughout the execution of the block in which they are declared. Although the values of these variables can be changed as the program executes, no program statement can create a new static variable or destroy an old one.

The trouble with static variables is that in some programs it is impossible to determine in advance how much memory will be needed. We would like to write programs in such a way that they can create variables when the variables are needed and dispose of them when they are no longer needed. The Pascal machine can recycle disposed-of memory locations and reuse them when new variables are created. Variables that are created and disposed of as the program executes are called *dynamic variables*.

Since a dynamic variable does not occur in a variable declaration, there is no identifier that we can use to refer to it. However, the routine that creates a dynamic variable returns the address of the memory location allocated. Such a memory address is called a *pointer*, since it designates or "points to" a particular memory location. To deal with dynamic variables, then, we need two things: (1) data types whose values are pointers, and (2) a mechanism for referring to a memory location that is designated by a pointer value.

We denote a pointer type by prefixing a type identifier with an upward arrow. The type identifier gives the type of variables that can be pointed to by values of the pointer type. Thus,

↑*integer*

is the data type whose values are pointers to integer variables and

↑*real*

is the data type whose values are pointers to real variables.

In hardware versions of Pascal, the upward arrow is often represented by a circumflex, ^. The types just given would be written as

^INTEGER   ^REAL

The declaration

p: ↑*integer*

specifies that the value of p is a pointer to a variable of type integer. To refer to the variable itself, we *follow* p with an upward arrow. Thus

$p\uparrow$

designates the variable pointed to by the value of p. We can treat $p\uparrow$ like any other integer variable. Thus

$p\uparrow := 25$

assigns 25 to the variable pointed to by the value of p, and

$i := p\uparrow$

assigns to i the value of the variable pointed to by the value of p.

It is often convenient to draw diagrams in which a pointer is represented by an arrow extending from the pointer variable to the variable being pointed to. Figure 11–1 uses such a diagram to illustrate the relationship between p and $p\uparrow$.

A standard procedure *new* creates a new variable. For instance,

$new(p)$

creates a new integer variable and assigns its address to p. The statement

$p\uparrow := 5$

assigns the value 5 to the newly created variable.

When a variable is no longer needed, the procedure *dispose* gives the Pascal machine the opportunity to mark the memory location for later reuse. Thus

$dispose(p)$

informs the Pascal machine that the variable pointed to by p will no longer be used.

FIGURE 11–1. In diagrams a pointer value is represented by an arrow. The arrow extends from inside the memory location holding the pointer value to the variable being pointed to. If p is the memory location holding the pointer value, $p\uparrow$ denotes the variable that is pointed to.

We occasionally need a pointer value that does not point to any variable. This value is represented by the reserved word **nil**. After the assignment

$p := $ **nil**

the value of p does not point to any variable. Therefore the expression $p\uparrow$ is meaningless when the value of p is **nil**.

Pointers to variables of simple types such as *integer* and *real* are rarely used. Usually we use pointers to point to records, which is why they are taken up in this chapter.

Suppose we want to represent a class roll as a list of records in the computer's memory, one record for each student. We want the list to be flexible so that we can easily delete the records of students who drop the class and insert new records for students who add the class.

We can achieve the flexibility we desire by using a *linked list*—a list in which the records for the different students are joined to one another by means of pointers.

For example, let us define the record type *student* as follows:

```
student = record
             name: packed array[1 . . 20] of char;
             grade: integer;
             link: ↑student
          end;
```

The value of the *link* field is a pointer to another student record, the next record on the list. For the last record on the list, the value of the link field is **nil**.

We can use a variable *first* declared by

first: ↑*student*

to point to the first record of the linked list. Figure 11–2 illustrates a linked list. The diagonal line across the link field of the last record stands for the value **nil**. The value **nil** is used as a sentinel to indicate the end of the list.

The first record on a linked list is different from all the others in that it is pointed to by the variable *first* rather than another record. This means that some

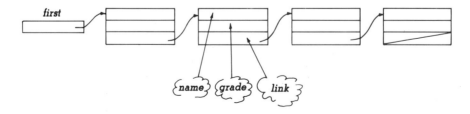

FIGURE 11-2. A linked list. The variable *first* points to the first record of the list. The link field of each record points to the following record. The link field of the last record has the value nil, which is indicated in the diagram by a diagonal line.

manipulations are different for the first record. To keep from always having to treat the first record as a special case, we begin the list with a dummy record called the *header* record, whose fields (other than the link field) are of no importance. By using the header, all the records that contain useful data are pointed to by the link fields of other records, and all can be treated in the same way.

Figure 11–3 shows a linked list with a header record. The *name* and *grade* fields are shaded to show that their values are of no importance. (Sometimes the header is used to contain information about the list as a whole, such as the number of records on it. For this purpose the header can be a variant of the records used on the rest of the list. In our examples, we will not use the header in this way.)

Now let us write a program to read in a series of student names and build a linked list of student records:

```
procedure readclass(first: ↑student);
var
    p, q: ↑student; i: integer;
begin
    new(p);                          {create header}
    first := p;                      {first points to header}
    while not eof(input) do
        begin
            new(q);                  {create a new record}
            p↑.link := q ;           {link new record to end of list}
            p := q ;                 {p points to new end of list}
            for i := 1 to 20 do      {read name}
                read(p↑.name[i]);
            readln                   {go to next line}
        end;
    p↑.link := nil;                  {link of last record is nil}
end
```

The statement

new(q)

creates a new record and assigns a pointer to it to *q*. The variable *p* currently points to the last record on the list. The crucial statement

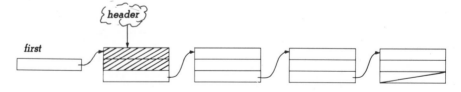

FIGURE 11–3. Since the first record of a linked list has to be treated as a special case in many operations, the first record is often made a dummy *header* record that contains no useful information. In the diagram the *name* and *grade* fields of the header are shaded to show that they are not used.

$p\uparrow.link := q$

causes the link field of the current last record to point to the newly created record. That is, the newly created record is added to the end of the list. The value of q is assigned to p

$p := q$

so that p once again points to the last record on the list. Figure 11–4 illustrates these three statements.

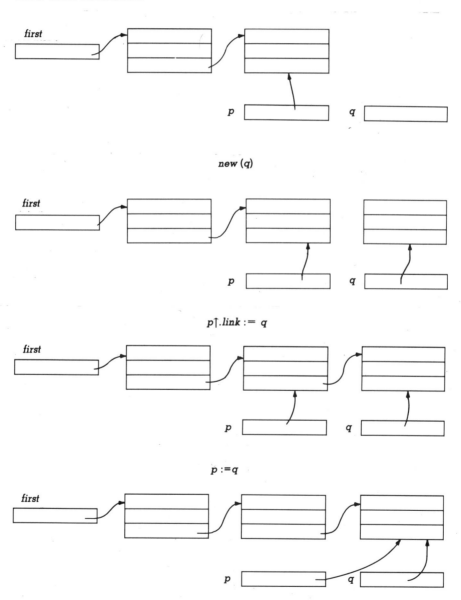

FIGURE 11-4. A new record is added to at the end of a linked list in three steps.

What remains to be done is to read a student's name into the *name* field of the newly created record. The reference in the *read* statement is interesting:

$p\uparrow$

is a record variable, the record variable pointed to by *p*;

$p\uparrow.name$

is an array variable, the *name* field of the record pointed to by *p*. Finally,

$p\uparrow.name[i]$

is an indexed variable whose value is the *i*th component of the *name* field of the variable pointed to by *p*. This variable is of type *char*, so

$read(p\uparrow.name[i])$

reads one character and assigns it to $p\uparrow.name[i]$.

After all the names have been read, the link field of the last record is set to **nil**. Note that no values have been assigned to the *grade* fields of the records. Contrary to student suspicions, final grades are not assigned when the class list is made out at the beginning of the semester.

Suppose we wish to insert a new record in the list. Let *p* point to the record preceding the point where the insertion is to be made. Figure 11–5 illustrates the insertion process.

We begin by creating a new record:

$new(q)$

The new record is to be inserted between $p\uparrow$ and the record following $p\uparrow$. Therefore, the link field of the new record should point to the record that now follows $p\uparrow$. That record is now pointed to by the link field of $p\uparrow$, so

$q\uparrow.link := p\uparrow.link$

Finally, the link field of $p\uparrow$ should be set to point to the newly created record:

$p\uparrow.link := q$

The value of *q* is returned for use in storing information in the newly inserted record. We can write a function *insert* that performs the insertion and returns a pointer to the inserted record:

function *insert*(*p*: ↑*student*): ↑*student*;
var
   q: ↑*student*;

begin
    new(q);
    q↑.link := p↑.link;
    p↑.link := q;
    insert := q
end

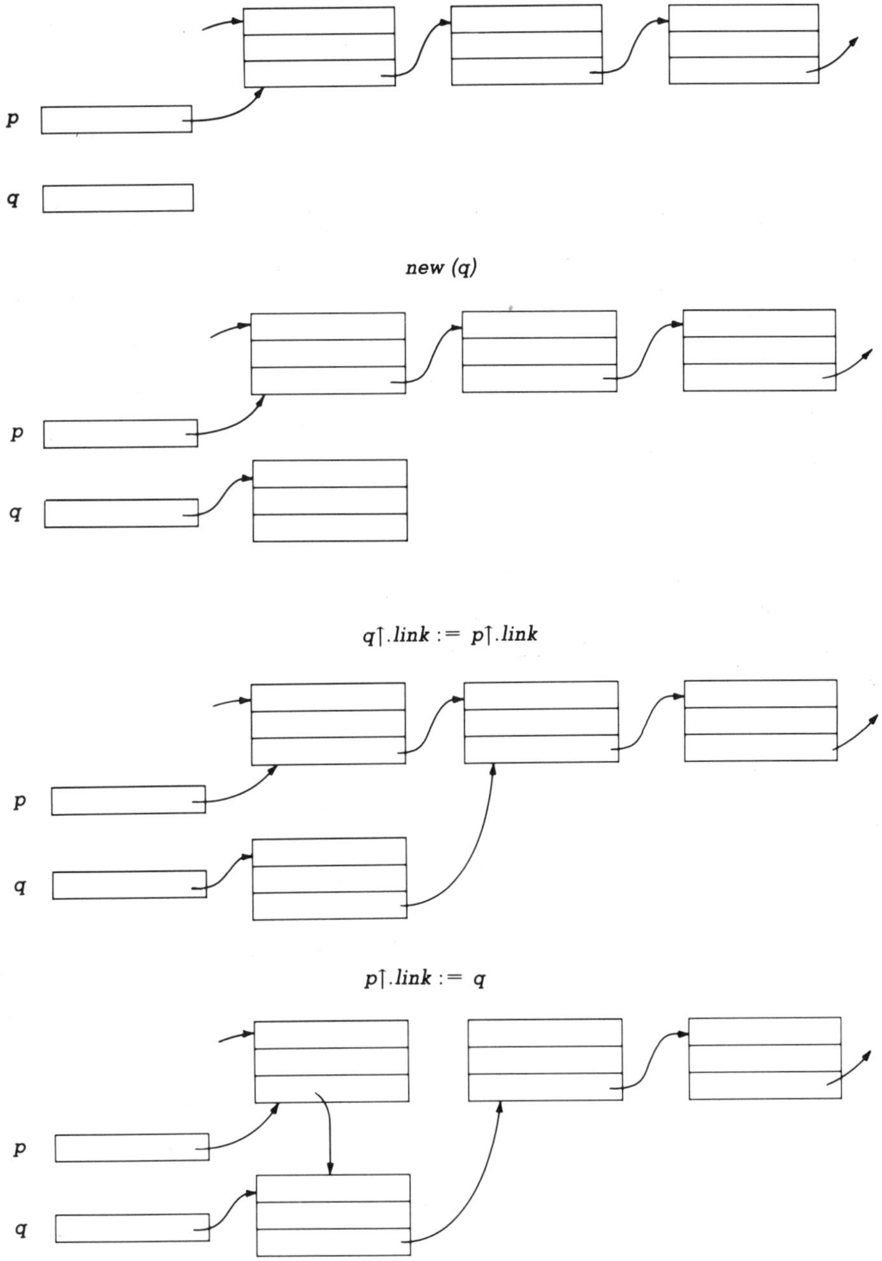

new (q)

q↑.link := p↑.link

p↑.link := q

FIGURE 11-5. Inserting a new record into a linked list. The new record is to be inserted following the record pointed to by *p*.

Now suppose we want to delete the record *following* the one pointed to by *p*. Figure 11–6 illustrates the procedure. We start by setting *q* to point to the record to be deleted:

$q := p\uparrow.link$

Next we link around the deleted record, so that *p↑.link* points to the record following the deleted record instead of to the deleted record:

$p\uparrow.link := q\uparrow.link$

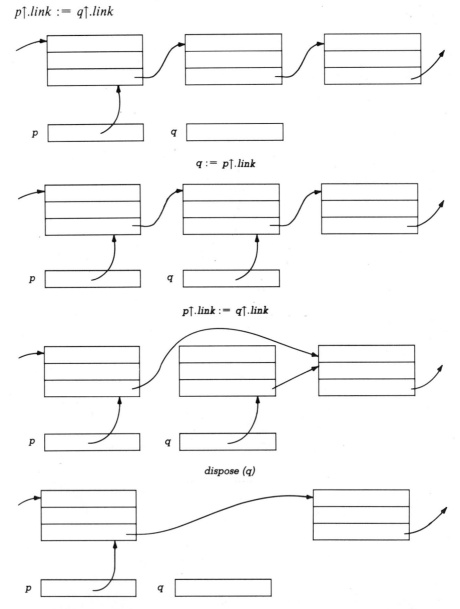

$q := p\uparrow.link$

$p\uparrow.link := q\uparrow.link$

dispose (q)

FIGURE 11–6. Deleting a record from a linked list. The record to be deleted is the one following the record pointed to by *p*.

Finally, we inform the Pascal machine that the record pointed to by *q* is available to be reused:

dispose(q)

The following procedure deletes the record following the one pointed to by the actual parameter *p*:

```
procedure delete(p: ↑student);
var
    q: ↑student;
begin
    q := p↑.link;
    p↑.link := q↑.link;
    dispose(q)
end
```

Suppose we wish to locate the record of a particular student to modify or delete it. To modify the record we need a pointer to that record. To delete the record we need a pointer to the preceding record. Hence our search procedure will return not only a pointer to the record found but a pointer to the preceding record as well:

```
procedure find(first: ↑student;
               vfind: packed array[1..20] of char;
               var p, q: ↑student);
var
    notfound: Boolean;
begin
    p := first;
    q := first↑.link;
    notfound := true;
    while (q <> nil) and notfound do
        if q↑.name = vfind then
            notfound = false
        else
            begin
                p := q;
                q := q↑.link
            end
end
```

When *find* returns, if the value of *q* is **nil** then the sought-after record was not found. If the value of *q* is not **nil**, then *q* points to a record whose *name* field is equal to *vfind* and *p* points to the preceding record.

It will be left as an exercise to work out the detailed operation of *find*. But note the following: It is tempting to write the **while** statement like this:

while (*q* <> **nil**) **and** (*q*↑.*name* <> *vfind*) **do**

This will not work, since if the value of q is **nil**, then $q\uparrow$ is not defined and a reference to $q\uparrow.name$ is an error. We must make sure that no reference to $q\uparrow$ is made when the value of q is **nil**. This is the reason for the flag *notfound*.

We note that the only pointer constant provided is **nil**. All other pointer values are created by the procedure *new*. Aside from the assignment operator, the only operators that can be applied to pointer values are the relational operators $=$ and $<>$.

EXERCISES

1. The idea of a stack was introduced in the preceding chapter. Let us define a data type *stack* by

```
stack := record
            top: integer;
            contents: array[1..50] of integer;
         end;
```

and declare s

```
s: stack;
```

When s is empty the value of $s.top$ is 0. Otherwise, $contents[s.top]$ contains the top value on the stack. When the value of $s.top$ is 50, the stack is said to be full. Write the following two predicates:

empty(s)   Returns *true* if s is empty;
                      otherwise returns *false*.

full(s)   Returns *true* if s is full;
                      otherwise returns *false*.

Now write the following three procedures for manipulating stacks:

clear(s)   Produces an empty stack by setting $s.top$ to 0.

push(s, i)   If *full*(s) is *false*, adds the value of i to the top of stack
                      s. Otherwise, leaves s unchanged.

pop(s, i)   If *empty*(s) is false, removes the top value from the stack
                      and assigns that value to i. Otherwise, leaves s and i
                      unchanged.

All valid manipulations of the stack can be carried out using the two predicates and the three procedures. When using those predicates and procedures, we do not have to know how the stack is implemented—that is, we do not have to know how the data type *stack* is defined.

2. To illustrate the remark made at the end of Exercise 1, let us implement a stack as a linked list and write the same predicates and procedures for this implementation. Although the internal workings of the predicates and procedures will be vastly different, they can be used in exactly the same way. We define the following two data types

item = **record**
　　　　value: *integer*;
　　　　link: ↑*item*
　　　end;
stack = ↑*item*;

and the variable

s: *stack*;

The value of *s* points to the top item on the stack. Each item is linked to the one immediately below it. The link field of the bottom item is **nil**. When the stack is empty, the value of *s* is **nil**. New values of type *item* are created by *new* when values are pushed on the stack and disposed of when values are popped off. Write the predicates *full* and *empty* and the procedures *clear*, *push*, and *pop*.

3. This problem is for readers familiar with complex numbers. Define a data type

complex = **record**
　　　　　r, *i*: real
　　　　end;

and variables

x, *y*, *z*: complex;

We intend for *x.r* to be the real part of the value of *x* and *x.i* is the imaginary part of the value of *x*. Write the following procedures:

sum(*x*, *y*, *z*)　　　　Sets *z* equal to the sum of
　　　　　　　　　　the complex numbers *x* and *y*.

diff(*x*, *y*, *z*)　　　　Sets *z* equal to the difference of
　　　　　　　　　　the complex numbers *x* and *y*.

prod(*x*, *y*, *z*)　　　　Sets *z* equal to the product of
　　　　　　　　　　the complex numbers *x* and *y*.

quot(*x*, *y*, *z*)　　　　Sets *z* equal to the quotient
　　　　　　　　　　of the complex numbers *x* and *y*.

4. Suppose the linked-list class roll described in the chapter is kept in alphabetical order on the students' names. Write a procedure that, given the name of a student who is adding the course, will find the point at which the new student's name should be inserted so as to keep the list in alphabetical order. The procedure should return a pointer to the record preceding the point at which the insertion should be made.

5. Why does the *delete* procedure require a pointer to the record *preceding* the one to be deleted?

6. In a doubly-linked list, each record contains not only a pointer to the record that follows it but a pointer to the record that precedes it as well. To make the class roll into a doubly-linked list, we could define *student* as follows:

```
student = record
            name: packed array[1..20] of char;
            grade: integer;
            leftlink,
            rightlink: ↑student
          end;
```

Write versions of *insert* and *delete* for doubly-linked lists. This version of *delete* should be provided with a pointer to the record to be deleted, not to the preceding record.

Chapter 12

STRUCTURED TYPES: FILES

A sequence of values stored in auxiliary memory is known as a *file*.

There are two kinds of file: *sequential* and *random*. The values in a sequential file can only be accessed in the order in which they are stored in auxiliary memory. The values in a random file (also called a *direct-access* file) can be accessed in any order desired by the programmer.

Standard Pascal, which was designed as a language for teaching programming, makes provisions only for sequential files. More and more, however, Pascal is being used in the real world outside of educational institutions. These real-world versions of Pascal must provide for random files, which are extremely important in practical applications.

In this chapter we will confine ourselves to the sequential files of standard Pascal. Usually, only minor additions are required to let the language handle random files as well.

A computer does not directly manipulate the values stored in auxiliary memory. Instead, the values must be transferred to main memory for manipulation. At any time, we can think of one value from a file as being in main memory and available for use. The remaining values are in auxiliary memory and not currently available.

We can think of a file as having a *window* through which exactly one value can be seen. The value seen through the window (the value in main memory) is accessible to us. The other values (the ones in auxiliary memory) are not currently accessible. For a file of integers, we can diagram this situation as follows:

5   7 | 1 | 8   2   5   9   6   3   4

The value seen through the window is in main memory and currently accessible. The remaining values are in auxiliary memory and currently inaccessible.

A file is declared as follows:

type
 data = **file of** *integer*;
var
 f: *data*;

Note that, like an array, the type of the components that can be stored in a file are specified. On the other hand, the size of the file is *not* specified. The size varies with the number of values that are actually stored in the file.

If *f* is a file variable then *f*↑ represents the window through which one value can be seen. We treat *f*↑ like a variable. That is, we obtain a value from the file by using *f*↑ in an expression

$$i := f\uparrow$$

and the first step in transferring a value to the file is to assign it to *f*↑:

$$f\uparrow := i$$

We call *f* the *buffer variable*, since the term buffer refers to an area of main memory that holds a value read from auxiliary memory or one that is to be written in auxiliary memory. We can diagram the file *f* and its buffer variable *f*↑ as follows:

5 7 | 1 | 8 2 5 9 6 3 4

   f↑

Files whose identifiers appear as parameters in the program heading are *external files*. These refer to existing files in auxiliary memory, such as a customer file or an employee file. Files whose identifiers do not appear as program parameters are *local files*; they do not correspond to any pre-existing files. The program uses local files for temporary storage.

STANDARD FILE-HANDLING PROCEDURES

Pascal provides a set of standard procedures for reading and writing files. These procedures are *reset*, *rewrite*, *get*, and *put*.

The procedure statement

reset(f)

positions the window *f*↑ at the beginning of the file:

| 5 | 7 1 8 2 5 9 6 3 4

f↑

The value of $f\uparrow$ is now 5—the first value in the file. We can access this value as follows:

$i := f\uparrow$

After the assignment, the value of i is 5.

The procedure statement

$get(f)$

moves the window forward one position:

5	7	1	8	2	5	9	6	3	4

$f\uparrow$

Now the statement

$i := f\uparrow$

assigns the value 7 to i. Executing

$get(f)$

again moves the window forward one more position

5	7	1	8	2	5	9	6	3	4

$f\uparrow$

and so on.

The expression

$eof(f)$

is *false* as long as the file window is positioned over a component of the file. When the file window moves beyond the end of the file, the value of $eof(f)$ becomes *true*.

For instance, after $get(f)$ has been executed a sufficient number of times, the file in our example will look like this:

5	7	1	8	2	5	9	6	3	4

$f\uparrow$

The value of $eof(f)$ is *false* and the value of $f\uparrow$ is 4. Now suppose $get(f)$ is executed again. The window is moved beyond the end of the file:

5	7	1	8	2	5	9	6	3	4	

$f\uparrow$

Now the value of *eof(f)* is *true* and the value of *f* ↑ is undefined. Furthermore, the effect of any further executions of *get(f)* is undefined.

The following illustrates the general form of the statements for reading and processing the values in file:

reset(f);
while not *eof(f)* **do**
   begin
       .
       .   *{statements using the value of f↑}*
       .
     get(f)
   end

For instance, we can compute the sum of the values in a file of integers as follows:

sum := 0
reset(f);
while not *eof(f)* **do**
   begin
      sum := *sum*+*f*↑;
      get(f)
   end

We can write a new value into the file only when the value returned by *eof* is *true*—that is, the file is either empty or the window has been moved past the last value. To write a new value in the file we assign the value to *f* ↑ and execute *put(f)*.

For instance, when we last left our example file it was in the following state

5   7   1   8   2   5   9   6   3   4   [   ]
                                      f↑

To add the value 7 to the end of the file, we execute

f↑ := 7

giving

5   7   1   8   2   5   9   6   3   4   [7]
                                        f↑

Executing

put(f)

moves the window forward one position, thereby appending 7 to the file stored in auxiliary memory:

5   7   1   8   2   5   9   6   3   4   7   ☐

$f\uparrow$

After *put(f)* is executed, the value of *eof(f)* is once again *true*, and the value of $f\uparrow$ is again undefined. Additional values can be appended to the file by repeating the process just described.

Although we can append additional values to the end of any existing file, the more common procedure is to start with an empty file. The statement

rewrite(f)

assigns an empty file to the file variable *f*. After this statement has been executed, we can visualize the file like this:

☐

$f\uparrow$

The values of *eof(f)* is true and we are ready to begin writing values into the file. For instance, suppose the statements

$f\uparrow := 3;$
put(f);
$f\uparrow := 5;$
put(f);
$f\uparrow := 7;$
put(f);

are executed. The file now looks like this:

3   5   7   ☐

$f\uparrow$

As a further example of writing into files, the following statements store the values 1 through 100 in a file of integers:

rewrite(f);
for $i := 1$ **to** 100 **do**
   begin
      $f\uparrow := i;$
      put(f)
   end

THE CLASSICAL FILE-UPDATE PROBLEM

Suppose we have a permanent file such as a file of customer accounts. Each month certain transactions take place, such as purchases, shipments, and payments. These transactions bring about changes in the customer accounts—each payment a customer makes, for instance, must be recorded in his account. Therefore, the file of customer accounts has to be updated monthly using the information about the transactions.

We call the file of customer accounts the *master file* and the file containing the information about the transactions the *transaction file*. We use the contents of the transaction file to update the master file.

Specifically, the master file that was produced last month is called the *old master file*. The old master file and the transaction file are used to produce a *new master file* containing up-to-date information. This month's new master file becomes next month's old master file.

Suppose that the records in the master file have the following form:

master = **record**
       key: **packed array**[1..9] **of** *char*;
       permanentdata: **packed array**[1..80] **of** *char*;
       updatedata: **packed array**[1..80] **of** *char*
    end;

The *key* field identifies the person (or other entity) to whom the record applies. It will normally be an account number.

The remaining fields depend on the purpose for which the file is being kept. For simplicity, we will use only two additional fields: *permanentdata*, which is not subject to being updated, and *updatedata*, which is subject to monthly change. In reality, we would have a large number of fields, some of which would be subject to update and some of which would not.

There are three kinds of transactions that can take place. We can add a new record to the file, we can update a record that is in the file, or we can delete a record that is in the file. Let us use a value of type *transtype* to distinguish the three kinds of transactions:

transtype = (*add*, *update*, *delete*);

Let the records in the transaction file have the following form:

trans = **record**
       key: **packed array**[1..9] **of** *char*;
       kind: *transtype*;
       permanentdata: **packed array**[1..80] **of** *char*;
       updatedata: **packed array**[1..80] **of** *char*
    end

Again, the *key* field identifies the person to whom the record applies. The *kind* field determines whether the transaction is *add*, *update*, or *delete*. The kind of transaction determines which of the remaining fields will be used. If we are adding a new record, both *permanentdata* and *updatedata* are used. If we are updating an existing record, only *updatedata* is used. If we are deleting a record, neither of these fields is used.

(We could use record variants so that the record for each transaction would contain only the fields necessary for that transaction. But this would complicate our example without providing any further insight. So we will settle for sometimes letting some of the fields be unused.)

Now suppose we have three files: *oldmaster*, *newmaster*, and *transaction*:

oldmaster, *newmaster*: **file of** *master*;
transaction: **file of** *trans*;

The records in the *oldmaster* and *transaction* files must be sorted into ascending order according to their key fields. The progam produces a *newmaster* file whose records are in ascending order according to their key fields.

In writing the file-update program, we will employ a variation of stepwise refinement that uses procedure statements in place of English descriptions. We write procedure statements to do jobs whose details we do not want to worry about at the moment. When we are ready to fill in the details, we write the procedures called by the procedure statements.

Using this method, we can outline the file-update program as follows:

reset(*oldmaster*);
reset(*transaction*);
rewrite(*newmaster*);
endfile := *eof*(*oldmaster*) **or** *eof*(*transaction*);
while not *endfile* **do**
    compareandprocess;
while not *eof*(*oldmaster*) **do**
    nextmaster;
while not *eof*(*transaction*) **do**
    add

We begin by resetting *oldmaster* and *transaction* and by preparing *newmaster* for rewriting. The Boolean variable *endfile* has the value *true* if the end of either *oldmaster* or *transaction* has been reached. Otherwise, the value of *endfile* is *false*. We give *endfile* the initial value *eof*(*oldmaster*) **or** *eof*(*transaction*).

We now compare the keys of the records read from the *newmaster* and *transaction* files; the results of the comparison determine the processing to be done. For the moment we will ignore the details of this processing entirely; we will just call a not-yet-written procedure, *compareandprocess*, to handle it. We execute *compareandprocess* repeatedly while there remain records to be processed in both the *oldmaster* and *transaction* files.

When the end of either the *newmaster* or the *transaction* file is reached, there will usually still be some records remaining to be processed in the other file. We use two **while** statements to handle these "left-over" records.

Suppose that the left-over records are in the *oldmaster* file. Since the transactions have all been processed, none of the remaining master records will be updated or deleted. Therefore, we move all the remaining records in the *oldmaster* file to the *newmaster* file. This is done by executing the procedure *nextmaster* while records remain in the *oldmaster* file. *Nextmaster* writes the current oldmaster record—the one seen through the file window—in the *newmaster* file and reads another record from the *oldmaster* file.

Suppose the *transaction* file contains the left-over records. These transactions cannot be updates or deletions, since there remain no master records to be updated or deleted. The transactions must represent new records to be added to the file. Therefore, the procedure *add*, which adds a record to the *newmaster* file, is executed for each remaining transaction.

Now let us turn to the procedure *compareandprocess*:

```
procedure compareandprocess;
begin
    if oldmaster↑.key < transaction↑.key then
        nextmaster
    else if oldmaster↑.key = transaction↑.key then
        updateordelete
    else
        add
end
```

The procedure *compareandprocess* compares the keys of the current *oldmaster* and *transaction* records—the ones currently visible through the file windows. Depending upon the result of the comparison, we have one of three possible cases:

Case 1   The key of the current *oldmaster* record is less than the key of the current *transaction* record. Since the files are in ascending order, neither the current *transaction* record nor any following it can have the same key as the current *oldmaster* record. Therefore, no further processing can be carried out on the current *oldmaster* record. We call *nextmaster* to write the current *oldmaster* record in the *newmaster* file and get the next *oldmaster* record.

Case 2   The keys of the current *oldmaster* and *transaction* records are the same. We have matched a *transaction* record with the corresponding *oldmaster* record. The only permissible operations are update and delete; we cannot add a record with the same key as a record already in the file. We call a procedure *updateordelete* to update or delete as required.

Case 3   The key of the current *oldmaster* record is greater than the key of the current *transaction* record. The key of the *transaction* record does not match the key of any *oldmaster* record, since it has not matched the keys of any of the *oldmaster* records already processed and it cannot match the key of any record remaining in the *oldmaster* file. Therefore this transaction must specify a new record to be added to the *newmaster* file; we call the procedure *add* to make the addition.

Now we have to write the procedures *nextmaster*, *updateordelete*, and *add*, which actually handle the records. The procedure *nextmaster* writes the current *oldmaster* record in the *newmaster* file and reads a new record from the *oldmaster* file:

```
procedure nextmaster;
begin
    newmaster↑ := oldmaster↑;
    put(newmaster);
    get(oldmaster);
    endfile := eof(oldmaster)
end
```

Note that if there are no *oldmaster* records remaining to be read, then the value of *endfile* is set to *true*.

The procedure *updateordelete* updates or deletes the current *oldmaster* record, depending upon the kind of transaction specified. If the *transaction* record erroneously requests an addition, a procedure *error* is called to inform the user of the erroneous transaction and to get a new *transaction* record:

```
procedure updateordelete;
begin
    case transaction↑.kind of
        add: error;
        update: begin
                    oldmaster↑.updatedata := transaction↑.updatedata;
                    get(transaction);
                    endfile := eof(transaction)
                end;
        delete: begin
                    get(oldmaster);
                    get(transaction);
                    endfile := eof(oldmaster) or eof(transaction);
                end
    end {case}
end
```

The procedure *add* uses the data in the *transaction* record to add a new record to the *newmaster* file:

```
procedure add;
begin
    if transaction↑.kind<> add then
        error
    else
```

```
        begin
            newmaster↑.key := transaction↑.key;
            newmaster↑.permanentdata := transaction↑.permanentdata;
            newmaster↑.updatedata := transaction↑.updatedata;
            put(newmaster);
            get(transaction);
            endfile := eof(transaction)
        end
end
```

The procedure *error* warns of an erroneous transaction and gets a new *transaction* record:

```
procedure error;
begin
    writeln('ERRONEOUS TRANSACTION: ', transaction↑.key);
    get(transaction);
    endfile := eof(transaction)
end
```

Now we are ready to bring all the parts together and write the complete file-update program:

```
program fileupdate(oldmaster, newmaster, transaction, output);
type
    transtype = (add, update, delete);
    master = record
                key: packed array[1..9] of char;
                permanentdata: packed array[1..80] of char;
                updatedata: packed array[1..80] of char
            end;
    trans = record
                key: packed array[1..9] of char;
                kind: transtype;
                permanentdata: packed array[1..80] of char;
                updatedata: packed array[1..80] of char
            end;
var
    oldmaster, newmaster: file of master;
    transaction: file of trans;
    endfile: Boolean;


procedure error;
begin
    writeln('ERRONEOUS TRANSACTION: ', transaction↑.key);
    get(transaction);
    endfile := eof(transaction)
end; {of error}
```

```
procedure nextmaster;
begin
    newmaster↑ := oldmaster↑;
    put(newmaster);
    get(oldmaster);
    endfile := eof(oldmaster)
end; {of newmaster}

procedure updateordelete;
begin
    case transaction↑.kind of
        add: error;
        update: begin
                    oldmaster↑.update := transaction↑.update;
                    get(transaction);
                    endfile := eof(transaction);
                end;
        delete: begin
                    get(oldmaster);
                    get(transaction);
                    endfile := eof(oldmaster) or eof(transaction);
                end
    end {case}
end; {of updateordelete}

procedure add;
begin
    if transaction↑.kind <> add then
        error
    else
        begin
            newmaster↑.key := transaction↑.key;
            newmaster↑.permanentdata := transaction↑.permanentdata;
            newmaster↑.updatedata := transaction↑. updatedata;
            put(newmaster);
            get(transaction);
            endfile := eof(transaction)
        end
end; {of add}

procedure compareandprocess;
begin
    if oldmaster↑.key < transaction↑.key then
        nextmaster
    else if oldmaster↑.key = transaction↑.key then
        updateordelete
    else
        add
end; {of compareandprocess}
```

```
begin {main program}
    reset(oldmaster);
    reset(transaction);
    rewrite(newmaster);
    endfile := eof(oldmaster) or eof(transaction);
    while not endfile do
        compareandprocess;
    while not eof(oldmaster) do
        nextmaster;
    while not eof(transaction) do
        add
end. {of fileupdate}
```

TEXTFILES

Files of characters are often divided up into lines. Pascal has a predefined file type *text* that recognizes this division. We can think of *text* as being defined by

text = **file of** *char*;

with the additional provision that the division of the file into lines is to be recognized. The standard files *input* and *output* are of type *text*.

We can think of a special line-separator character being used to divide the textfile into lines. Let us denote that character by a vertical bar, |. then if our textfile consists of the three lines

```
112345 25.1   35.42
230987 42.4   15.76
277890 28.3   12.35
```

we can visualize it like this:

112345 25.1   35.42|230987 42.4   15.76|277890 28.3   12.35

At first thought it might seem that the best thing to do is to let the program read the line separator just like any other character. We could then write our program to use the line separator as an end-of-line sentinel.

Unfortunately, different Pascal machines use different line separator characters. If we wrote our program to recognize a particular line-separator character, then it would work on some Pascal machines but not on others.

To keep our programs from being dependent on a particular line-separator character, Pascal does the following:

1. When the file window is a over a line-separator character, Pascal assigns a blank space to the buffer variable. Thus the line-separator character looks like a blank space to a program.

2. To let the program detect the end of a line, the predicate *eoln* is provided. The expression *eoln(f)* is *true* when the file window of *f* is over a line separator and *false* otherwise.

The blank corresponding to the line-separator character usually causes the program no trouble, since programs that process text have to be able to handle blank spaces anyway. So if we wish we can ignore the division of the file into lines. When we need to know when the end of a line has been reached, we can use the predicate *eoln*.

Standard Procedures

Since textfiles are very widely used, Pascal provides additional standard procedures for manipulating them. These are just the procedures *read*, *readln*, *write*, and *writeln* that we have been using all along. With our present knowledge of files we can define these procedures somewhat more precisely.

Let c be a character variable and f a file variable. Then

$read(f, c)$

is equivalent to

$c := f\uparrow;$
$get(f)$

and

$write(f, c)$

is equivalent to

$f\uparrow := c;$
$put(f)$

that is, $read(f, c)$ assigns to c the character of f currently visible through the file window and then moves the window forward one character. The statement $write(f, c)$ appends the value of c to the end of file f.

The procedure *read* is defined for variables of type *integer* and *real* as well as *char*. If v is a variable of type *integer* or *real*, then

$read(f, v)$

reads an integer or real number (depending on the type of v) from f and assigns its value to v. The procedure will skip preceding blank spaces to get to the integer or real number; when the procedure returns, the file window is positioned over the first character following the integer or real number.

If *e* is an expression of type *integer*, *real*, *Boolean*, or packed array of *char*, then

write(f, e)

causes the value of *e* to be converted to character form and the characters to be appended to file *f*. As we have discussed before, field-width parameters can be used to control the form of the printed value.

The *read* and *write* procedures can read or write more than one value in a single call. The statement

read(f, v1, v2, . . ., vn)

is defined to be equivalent to

read(f, v1);
read(f, v2);
　.
　.
　.
read(f, vn)

and

write(f, e1, e2, . . ., en)

is equivalent to

write(f, e1);
write(f, e2);
　.
　.
　.
write(f, en)

The procedure *readln* moves the file window to the character following the next line separator. Thus

readln(f)

is equivalent to

while not *eoln(f)* **do**
　get(f);
get(f)

The procedure *writeln* appends a line separator to the file being written. After

writeln(f)

the next character written will start a new line.

The procedures *readln* and *writeln* can be combined with *read* and *write*. Thus

readln(f, v1, v2, ..., vn)

is equivalent to

read(f, v1, v2, ..., vn);
readln

and

writeln(f, e1, e2, ..., en)

is equivalent to

write(f, e1, e2, ..., en);
writeln

THE FILES input AND output

Because of the importance and frequent use of the standard files *input* and *output*, there are some special rules regarding them:

1. The variables *input* and *output* are predeclared as follows:

input, output: text;

Declarations for these files must *not* be included in the program.

2. The procedures *reset* and *rewrite* must *not* be applied to *input* and *output*. Before the beginning of program execution the following operations are, in effect, performed by the Pascal machine:

reset(input);
rewrite(output)

3. If the file parameter is omitted for *read, readln, eof* or *eoln, input* is assumed. If the file parameter is omitted for *write* or *writeln, output* is assumed. Thus in the following the statements on the left and those on the right are equivalent:

read(v1, v2, ..., vn)	*read(input, v1, v2, ..., vn)*
readln(v1, v2, ..., vn)	*readln(input, v1, v2, ..., vn)*
eof	*eof(input)*
eoln	*eoln(input)*
write(e1, e2, ..., en)	*write(output, e1, e2, ..., en)*
writeln(e1, e2, ..., en)	*writeln(output, e1, e2, ..., en)*

The *read, readln, write,* and *writeln* statements on the left are, of course, just the ones that we have been using all along.

EXERCISES

1. A *listing* results when the contents of a file are printed out for easier reading. For instance, we may wish to print data that is punched on cards. Write a program to list the file *input* on *output*—that is, each line of input is to be printed as a line of output. The program should work regardless of the number of characters on a line or the number of lines in *input*.

2. Write a program similar to that of Exercise 1 except that each printed line is to be preceded by a *line number*. The line number will be printed in a four-character field and will be separated from the remainder of the line by one blank space. The first line printed will be numbered 1, the next line, will be numbered 2, and so on.

3. Suppose the file *class* is declared as follows:

type
    student = **record**
                id: **packed array**[1..9] **of** *char*;
                name: **packed array**[1..40] **of** *char*;
                grade: *integer*
          end:
var
    class: **file of** *student*;

Write a program to print a listing of the file *class*.

4. The records in the file *class* are supposed to be in order of increasing values of the *id* field. Write a program to check the order of the records in *class* and print the *id* fields of any exceptions. Specifically, the program will print the *id* field of any record whose *id* field is less than that of some preceding record.

5. Suppose that two classes are to be combined. We want to *merge* the files *class1* and *class2* into a single file, *class3*, where

class1, *class2*, *class3*: **file of** *student*;

The records of *class1* and *class2* are in ascending order according to the value of the *id* field, and *class3* should be likewise. *Hints*: A merge program is similar to, but simpler than, the file update program discussed in the chapter. On each cycle the program compares *class1*↑.*id* and *class2*↑.*id*. If

class1↑.*id* < *class2*↑.*id*

the the value of *class1*↑ is written in *class3*. Otherwise, the value of *class2*↑ is written in *class3*. When the end of either *class1* or *class2* is reached, all the records remaining in the other file are transferred to *class3*.

Chapter 13

STRUCTURED TYPES: SETS

A *set* is a collection of values. For example, the set that contains the values 1, 3, 5, and 9 is denoted in Pascal as follows:

[1, 3, 5, 9]

The values that belong to a set are called its *elements*. The elements of [1, 3, 5, 9] are 1, 3, 5, and 9.

(If you have encountered sets in mathematics courses, you recall the elements were enclosed in braces, like this:

{1, 3, 5, 9}

In Pascal, however, braces are reserved for enclosing comments. Therefore, square brackets are used for sets.)

SET DECLARATIONS

A set type can be declared as follows:

letterset = **set of** 'A'..'Z';

The type 'A'..'Z' is called the *base type* and is the type of the elements of the sets. Suppose we declare

s: *letterset*;

then some possible values of *s* are

['A']   ['A', 'C']   ['A', 'E', 'I', 'O', 'U']   []

Notice that [] denotes the empty set, the set that has no elements. Every set type includes the empty set as a value, regardless of the base type.

Consider the following definitions

primary = (*red, yellow, blue*);
primset = **set of** *primary*;

The following are the possible values of type *primset*:

[] [*red*]   [*yellow*]   [*blue*]   [*red, yellow*]
[*red, blue*]   [*yellow, blue*]   [*red, yellow, blue*]

A variable of type *primset* must have one of these eight values.

The base type must be a simple type other than *real*. Each Pascal machine places certain additional limitations on values of set type. These limitations typically take the following form:

1. There is a limit on the number of elements a set can have. This in turn imposes a limit on the number of different values in the base type. A type can be the base type of a set only if the number of values belonging to it does not exceed a certain limit. This limit invariably excludes *integer* as a base type and may exclude *char* as well.

2. Only integers belonging to a certain subrange may be elements of sets. For instance, if the subrange is $0..58$, then $1..5$, $10..50$, and $0..58$ are permissible base types, but $-1..3$ and $98..100$ are not. Also the set [25, 40] is allowed but [−2, 5] and [59] are not.

3. If *char* is not allowed as a base type, then only character values belonging to some given subrange of *char* may be elements of sets.

If these restrictions were the same for every Pascal machine, they would not be too much of a problem. But since they are different for different machines, a program using sets may execute on one Pascal machine but not on another. This limits the usefulness of sets for programs that must run on more than one Pascal machine.

OPERATIONS ON SETS

Set values are created by means of *set constructors*. We have been using set constructors all along to display set values:

[1, 3, 5, 9]   ['A', 'B', 'C']   [*red, yellow*]

A set constructor is an expression that is evaluated as the program executes. This means that it can contain variables as well as constants. For instance, suppose that the variables i and j have the values 5 and 3. Then the set constructor

$[i, j, i+j, i-j, i*j, i \text{ div } j]$

has the value

$[5, 3, 8, 2, 15, 1]$

(The order in which the elements are listed is immaterial.) On the other hand, if the values of i and j were 7 and 2, the same set constructor would have the value

$[7, 2, 9, 5, 14, 3]$

The element list can contain subranges as well as the values of individual elements. Thus

$[1..5]$

is equivalent to

$[1, 2, 3, 4, 5]$

and

$['A', 'C'..'F', 'L', 'W'..'Z']$

is equivalent to

$['A', 'C', 'D', 'E', 'F', 'L', 'W', 'X', 'Y', 'Z']$

There are three operations that can be applied to sets to yield other sets. These are *union*, *intersection*, and *difference*, which are denoted in Pascal by the operators $+$, $*$, and $-$. They are defined as follows, when s and t are variables of the same set type:

$s+t$ The *union* of s and t, which consists of those elements that belong to s, t, or to both s and t.

$s*t$ The *intersection* of s and t, which consists of those elements that belong to both s and t.

$s-t$ The *difference* of s and t, which consists of those elements that belong to s but do not belong to t.

The following expressions and their values illustrate the union, intersection, and difference operations:

Expression	Value
[1, 2, 3] + [4, 5, 6]	[1, 2, 3, 4, 5, 6]
[1, 2, 3, 4] + [3, 4, 5]	[1, 2, 3, 4, 5]
[1, 2, 3, 4] * [3, 4, 5]	[3, 4]
[1, 2, 3] * [4, 5, 6]	[]
[1, 2, 3, 4, 5] − [2, 3]	[1, 4, 5]
[1, 2, 3] − [4, 5, 6]	[1, 2, 3]

The priorities of +, *, and − are the same when they are used as set operators as when they are used as arithmetic operators. Thus, the expression

[1, 2]*[2, 3]+[1, 5]*[5, 6]

is evaluated as follows:

[1, 2]*[2, 3]+[1, 5]*[5, 6]   {intersections first}
        [2]+[5]   {then union}
        [2, 5]

Parentheses can be used in set expressions, of course, as the following evaluation illustrates:

[1, 2]*([2, 3]+[1, 5])*[5,6]   {parentheses first}
[1, 2]*[1, 2, 3, 5]*[5, 6]   {left-to-right order}
        [1, 2]*[5, 6]
        []

The following relational operators may be applied to the sets of the same set type and yielding *Boolean* values:

=   <>
<=   >=
in

If *s* and *t* are set variables with the same base type, and the type of *i* is the same as the base type of *s* and *t*, we can define the relational operators as follows:

s = *t*   *true* if *s* *equals* *t*; that is, if *s* and *t* have the same elements

s <> *t*   *true* if *s* is *not equal* to *t*; that is, if *s* and *t* do not have the same elements

s <= t   *true* if *s* is a *subset* of *t*; that is, if every element of *s* is also an element of *t*

$s >= t$ *true* if s is a *superset* of t of t; that is, if every element of t is
                  also an element of s.

i **in** s *true* if the value of i is an *element* of s

The following expressions and values illustrate the relational operators for
sets:

Expression	Value
$[1, 2, 3] = [1, 2, 4]$	*false*
$[1, 2, 3] <> [1, 2, 4]$	*true*
$[2, 3] <= [1, 2, 3]$	*true*
$[1, 2, 3] >= [2]$	*true*
$[1, 2, 3] <= [1, 2, 4]$	*false*
$[1, 2, 3] >= [1, 2, 4]$	*false*
2 **in** $[1, 2, 3]$	*true*
4 **in** $[1, 2, 3]$	*false*

The relational operators all have the same priority, and that priority is the
same as the priority of the operators

$$= \qquad <> \qquad <= \quad >=$$

when they are applied to arithmetic expressions. Thus the relational operators
have a lower priority than $+$, $*$, or $-$. This means that in expressions such as

$s + t <= u*v$
i **in** $s + t - u$

the set expressions are evaluated before applying the relational operators.

USING SETS

We often use sets to avoid using complex *Boolean* expressions. For instance,
suppose that c is a character variable and we want to know whether the value of c
is one of the arithmetic operators $'+'$, $'-'$, $'*'$, or $'/'$. One way to determine this
would be to use the Boolean expression

$(c = '+')$ **or** $(c = '-')$ **or** $(c = '*')$ **or** $(c = '/')$

A much simpler expression that gives the same result is

c **in** $['+', '-', '*', '/']$

Or suppose we want to know if the value of c is one of the uppercase letters of
the alphabet. The expression

$('A' <= c)$ **and** $(c <= 'Z')$

would determine this, but the equivalent expression using sets

c **in** $['A'..'Z']$

is easier to read and can be evaluated more efficiently by the computer.

In several programs we have used a *flag*—a Boolean variable—to record whether or not a certain condition is true. One part of the program assigns a value to the flag and another part uses this value.

In a complex program we may have many conditions whose truth or falseness can influence the behavior of the program. Certain parts of the program may record that particular conditions are true or false. Other parts of the program will base their actions on the truth or falseness of the various conditions. For a particular action to be taken, certain conditions have to be true and other conditions have to be false. The truth or falseness of still other conditions may be irrelevant to the decision.

Suppose that for a particular program we are concerned with six conditions, which will denote a, b, c, d, e, and f. Let us define a data type whose values are those six conditions:

condition $= (a, b, c, d, e, f)$;

We will use a set t to record which conditions are true. At any time during the program, the conditions that are members of t are true and those that are not members of t are false. We declare t by

t: **set of** *condition*;

At the beginning of the program we assign to t the set of conditions that are initially true. Suppose that initially none of the conditions are true. Then we assign to t the empty set:

$t := []$

If a certain part of the program determines that the condition a is true, then it can add that condition to the set t of true conditions as follows:

$t := t + [a]$

If the value of t is $[c, f]$ before executing this statement, then it will be $[a, c, f]$ afterward. On the other hand, if the value of t is $[a, c, f]$ before executing the statement, then it will still be $[a, c, f]$ afterward.

Suppose another part of the program determines that condition a is false. It removes a from the set of true conditions as follows:

$t := t - [a]$

If the value of t is $[a, c, f]$ before executing this statement, it will be $[c, f]$ afterward. On the other hand, if the value of t is $[c, f]$ before executing the statement, then it still will be $[c, f]$ afterward.

Now suppose we want to execute a certain statement, $s1$, under the following conditions:

a and c are true
f is false
b, d, and e are irrelevant to the decision

Our first step is to eliminate from t the conditions whose truth are irrelevant to the decision. We can do this using the expression

$t*[a, c, f]$

The set $[a, c, f]$ is sometimes called a *mask*, since intersecting it with t masks or hides any elements of t whose presence is not relevant to the decision at hand.

In order for the statement to be executed, a and c must be elements of t and f must not be an element of t. That is, $s1$ is to be executed if

$t*[a, c, f] = [a, c]$

The following statement controls the execution of $s1$.

if $t*[a, c, f] = [a, c]$ **then**
    $s1$

We could write this in a more general form by using set variables m (the mask) and mt (the set of conditions that must be true). (The set of conditions that must be false is $m-mt$.) The statement controlling the execution of $s1$ becomes:

if $t*m = mt$ **then**
    $s1$

If the values of m and mt are $[a, c, f]$ and $[a, c]$ respectively, then the conditions for the execution of $s1$ will be the ones previously given. But suppose another part of the program makes the assignment:

$m := [a, b, c, d]$;
$mt := [a, b]$

Now $s1$ will be executed when a and b are true, and c and d are false. The conditions e and f are irrelevant.

Thus one part of a program can change the conditions under which a statement will be executed in another part of the program. This is an effect that is not easy to obtain with Boolean variables.

Now let us look at another application. In Chapter 1 we spoke of a *translator*, a program that inputs a program in a higher level language and outputs that program translated into another language.

The input to a translator is a stream of characters. The first step in the processing is to break this stream down into meaningful groupings of characters —reserved words, identifiers, numbers, operators, and the like. These groupings are called *symbols*, and we pick them out automatically when we read a program. For instance, when we see the statement

newval := *oldval* + 32**i*

we see not a stream of characters but a sequence of symbols:

newval
:=
oldval
+
32
*
i

The part of the translator that breaks a program down into its individual symbols is called a *scanner*.

Let us write a scanner that will input a simplified Pascal program and produce a list of symbols such as the one just shown. To simplify matters, we will assume that the Pascal program deals only with integers—only integer constants and operators applicable to integers appear. Also we will assume that there are no comments, and that the program is typed in all uppercase letters.

In writing the program we distinguish three kinds of symbols:

1. *Identifiers and reserved words.* We do not distinguish between identifiers and reserved words. (In a real translator a table of reserved words would be used to make the distinction.) For an identifier or reserved word, the first character must belong to ['A'..'Z'] and the remaining characters must belong to ['A'..'Z', '0'..'9'].

2. *Integer constants.* The characters of an integer constant must belong to ['0'..'9']. A plus or minus sign preceding a constant is considered to be a separate symbol, not part of the constant.

3. *Operators and punctuation marks*, such as +, −, *, :=, (, <=, and so on. The characters making up these all belong to

['+', '−', '*', '/', '=', '<', '>', '(', ')', ':', ';', ',', '[', ']']

The symbols of a program can be separated by any number of blank spaces. When two symbols of the same kind occur in succession, such as in

I := J DIV K;
J := +25

then they must be separated by at least one blank space.

In the program we assume that *char* may be used as a base type for sets:

```
program scan(input, output);
var
    c: char;
    special: set of char;
    scanning: Boolean;
begin
    special := ['+', '-', '*', '/', '=', '<', '>', '(', ')', ':', ';', ',', '[', ']'];
    scanning := true;
    read(c);
    while scanning do
        begin
            while c = ' ' do {skip blanks}
                read(c);
            if c in ['A'..'Z'] then {reserved word or identifier}
                begin
                    repeat
                        write(c);
                        read(c)
                    until not (c in ['A'..'Z', '0'..'9']);
                    writeln
                end
            else if c in ['0'..'9'] then {integer}
                begin
                    repeat
                        write(c);
                        read(c)
                    until not (c in ['0'..'9']);
                    writeln
                end
            else if c in special then {sign}
                begin
                    repeat
                        write(c);
                        read(c)
                    until not (c in special);
                    writeln
                end
            else if c = '.' then {the end}
                begin
                    writeln(c);
                    scanning := false
                end
            else {garbage}
                begin
                    writeln('ILLEGAL CHARACTER:  ', c);
                    read(c)
                end
        end {while}
end. {scan}
```

EXERCISES

1. Modify *scan* so that it ignores comments. When a '{' is encountered, every-thing through the next '}' is ignored. (This problem is slightly harder if '(*' and '*)' are used to enclose comments.)

2. Modify *scan* so that it will recognize string constants as separate symbols and print each string constant on a separate line. Assume that quote marks cannot occur inside string constants.

3. Same as Exercise 2, but assume that a quote mark is represented inside a string constant by two quote marks in succession. The two quote marks are to be printed as a single quote. That is, 'Y' 'ALL COME' is to be printed as Y'ALL COME. For this kind of problem, it is often helpful to look ahead one character, and Pascal provides a simple method for doing this. The value of *input*↑ is the next character that will be read.

4. Modify *scan* so that it will recognize real numbers as well as integer constants. A numeric constant will have the following general form: an integer part such as

254

followed by an optional fractional part such as

.75

followed by an optional exponent part such as

E + 25   or   E − 25   or   E25

5. Write a program that reads English text and prints a list of words making up the text in the order they occur. For instance, if the program reads

HELLO, HOW ARE YOU?

it prints

HELLO
HOW
ARE
YOU

The text may be punctuated with commas, semicolons, periods, exclamation points, and quotation marks. These punctuation marks should not be printed. But apostrophes are considered to be parts of words and are printed with the words.

APPENDIX 1:
PASCAL RESERVED WORDS

and	end	nil	set
array	file	not	then
begin	for	of	to
case	function	or	type
const	goto	packed	until
div	if	procedure	var
do	in	program	while
downto	label	record	with
else	mod	repeat	

APPENDIX 2:
THE goto STATEMENT

Programming in Pascal is done with constructions intended to accomplish specific purposes, such as the **if** and **case** statements for selection, the **for**, **while**, and **repeat** statements for repetition, and function and procedure definitions for providing building blocks from which to construct a program.

Upon rare occasions we may desire to have the computer leave one of these constructions before reaching its end. For this purpose, Pascal provides the **goto** statement, which causes the computer to jump to some other part of the program; execution continues from the part to which the computer jumps.

The following example illustrates the **goto** statement:

   goto 25;
     .
     .
     .
25: $i := 5$;
     .
     .
     .

The integer 25 is a *label*. The label is separated from the statement by a colon:

25: $i := 5$

The statement $i := 5$ is given the label 25.

When the computer executes

goto 25

it immediately goes to the statement labeled 25 and executes that statement. Execution continues from this point, with the statement following statement 25 executed next, the one after that next, and so on.

A label must be declared in the block in which it is used to label a statement. The declaration has the following form:

label 25;

A more complete form of our example, then, is the following:

label 25;

.

.

.

begin

.

.

.

   goto 25;

.

.

.

25: $i := 5$;

.

.

.

end

A label can only be used to label one statement (otherwise, the computer would not know which statement to go to). A label is an unsigned integer constant of up to four digits. Do not confuse the labels used with **goto** statements with the labels for the different cases in a **case** statement. The two kinds of labels are completely different. It is not permitted to jump *into* a structure such as an **if**, **case, for, while, repeat** statement or a function or procedure definition. It is permissible to jump *out* of such a structure, as the following examples illustrate.

Label declarations precede all the other declarations and definitions at the beginning of a block. The following shows the order of all the declarations and definitions permitted in Pascal:

label declarations
constant definitions
type definitions
variable declarations
function and procedure declarations

The following two examples illustrate ways in which the **goto** statement is sometimes used.

For the first example, consider the procedure *find* described in section 11.6. We can write a slightly shorter version of *find* using the **goto** statement:

```
procedure findl (first: ↑student;
              vfind: packed array[1 . . 20] of char;
              var p, q: ↑student);
label 1;
begin
    p := first;
    q := first↑.link;
    while q <> nil do
        begin
            if q↑.name = vfind then
                goto 1;
            p := q;
            q := q↑.link
        end;
1:
end
```

Notice that 1 labels a null statement, a statement which contains no commands for the computer. This is permitted. Also notice the semicolon following the **end** preceding the label. This semicolon separates the **while** statement from the null statement; it would not be used if the statement label were not present.

The advantage of *findl* over *find* is that *findl* does not have to check the Boolean variable *notfound* once each repetition. Thus a little time is saved, an amount that will be negligible in most cases. The disadvantage of *findl* is that it is harder to read, since the **while** statement lies to us. The **while** statement will be repeated while $q <> $ **nil**. But when we actually read the compound statement, we see that this is a lie, and the repetition will actually be terminated as soon as the sought-after value is found.

Saving time should not be used as an excuse for **goto** statements unless experiments performed using the computer prove that the time saved is significant. When a program executes too slowly, we usually need to use an entirely different approach to the problem, such as using Shellsort or Quicksort in place of Bubblesort.

A procedure or a function is called to carry out a particular operation. Sometimes the procedure or function finds that, due to conditions beyond its control, it is unable to complete the operation for which it was called. In that case a **goto** statement is sometimes used to escape from the procedure or function and terminate the program (or the part of it which is having trouble).

Suppose we have a program that processes input character by character. A procedure statement

getchar(c)

gets the next character from the input file and assigns it to the character variable *c*.

The input is supposed to be terminated by a sentinel, such as the character '.' that terminates a Pascal program. In normal operation, the program that calls *getchar* will detect the presence of the sentinel, realize there is no more input, and terminate its operations gracefully.

But suppose that the part of the input that contains the sentinel is inadvertently omitted. Then when *getchar* is called it will find that there are no more characters to be gotten. Since *getchar* can no longer perform the function for which it was called, there is little purpose for it to return to the point in the program from which it was called.

We can write *getchar* like this:

```
label 99;
var
    ch: char;
    .
    .
    .

procedure getchar(var c: char);
begin
    if eof(input) then
        begin
            writeln('UNEXPECTED END OF FILE');
            goto 99
        end
    else
        begin
            c := input↑;
            get(input)
        end
end;

begin      {main program}
    .
    .
    .

    getchar(ch);
    .
    .
    .

99:
end.
```

When *getchar* finds that the end of the file has been reached, it prints an error message and jumps to the end of the main program, thus terminating its execution. While this use of the **goto** statement is perhaps a bit more justified than the one in the preceding example, we could certainly envision other solutions to the problem. For instance, when *getchar* discovers the end of the file it could return a special end-of-file character reserved for that purpose. The main program could process the end-of-file character using the same selection structure that it uses for the other characters.

As a rule, **goto** statements make a program harder to read, understand, and debug. They should be used only as a last resort, when no other Pascal statement will do the job.

APPENDIX 3:
DECLARATIONS ASSUMED
IN THE TEXT

When the variables x, y, z, i, j, k, p, q, and c appear in examples that are not parts of the complete programs, the following declarations are assumed to apply:

var
 x, y, z: *real*;
 i, j, k: *integer*;
 p, q: *Boolean*;
 c: *char*;

FOR FURTHER READING

Bowles, Kenneth L. *Microcomputer Problem Solving Using PASCAL*. New York: Springer-Verlag, 1977.

Conway, R., Gries, D., and Zimmerman, E. C. *A Primer on PASCAL*. Cambridge, Mass: Winthrop Publishers, 1976.

Grogono, Peter. *Programming in PASCAL*. Reading, Mass: Addison-Wesley Publishing Company, 1978.

Jensen, Kathleen; and Wirth, Niklaus. *PASCAL User Manual and Report*. Berlin: Springer-Verlag, 1974.

Schneider, G. M., Weingart, S. W., and Perlman, D. M. *An Introduction to Programming and Problem Solving with PASCAL*. New York: John Wiley & Sons, 1978.

Wirth, Niklaus. *Systematic Programming*. Englewood Cliffs, N. J.: Prentice-Hall, 1973.

_____. *Algorithms + Data Structures = Programs*. Englewood Cliffs, N. J.: Prentice-Hall, 1976.

INDEX

A

Absolute value function, 56
abs (standard function), 56
Accumulating totals, 36-37
Accumulator, 37
Actual parameter, 54ff.
add (procedure), 207-208
Address, memory, 5
alarm (procedure), 116
Algorithm, blackjack dealer's, 74-78
Alternation (*see* Selection)
and, 52
Applications software, 6
Area, calculation of, 47-48
Arithmetic in Pascal, 23-26
Arithmetic operators, 24ff.
array, 122
Arrays, 121-145
   and **for** statements, 125-126, 139ff.
   assignment to, 128
   input and output of, 129-130
   multidimensional, 138-145
   one-dimensional, 121-138
   packed, 131-135
   two-dimensional, 138-145
Array types (*see* Arrays)
Array variable, 123, 125
Arrow
   in buffer variable, 200
   in pointer types and variables, 187ff.
ASCII, collating sequence for, 50-51
Assembly language, 7-8

Assignment, 32-37
   of arrays, 128
   of records, 177
Assignment operator, 32
Assignment statement, 32
Assumed declarations, 31
average (function), 127

B

BASIC, 8
Becomes (assignment operator), 32
begin, 22
   use with **for** statement, 60-61
Binary codes, 2-4
Binary digits, 2
Binary mileage indicator, 3
Binary notation, 3-4
Binary search, 150-154
   performance of, 151-152
binarysearch (procedure), 151
Bits, 2
Blackjack dealer's algorithm, 74-78
Block, 96-102
book (record), 178
Book, three dimensional array as, 139
Boolean constants, 14
Boolean expressions, 48-54
   in **if** statement, 72ff.
   in **repeat** statement, 68, 69
   in **while** statement, 65
Boolean operators, 52-54
   priorities of, 52

Boolean (standard data type), 14, 112, 114
Boolean values, printing, 19
box (procedure), 95
Braces
    for enclosing comments, 21-22
    for enclosing sets in mathematics, 215
Brackets
    for enclosing array indices, 123ff.
    for enclosing sets, 215ff.
Bubblesort, 155-160
Bubblesort (procedure), 157
Bubblesrt (procedure), 159
Buffer, 200
Buffer variable, 200

C

Card readers, 5
car (record), 177
case, 78, 84-86
    in records, 182-184
case statement, scalar data types in, 118
Central processing unit, 4, 5
Change-making program, 135-138
Character constants, 15
Character, line separator, 210ff.
Characters, printing, 19-20
char (data type), 14-15
chessman (data type), 112ff., 124-125
chr (standard function), 115-116
Circumflex, 187
clr (function), 117
COBOL, 8
Collating sequence, 50-51
Colon
    in declarations, 30
    in output statements, 17ff.
color (data type), 112ff., 130-131
Columns, of two-dimensional arrays, 139
Commas, not allowed in Pascal numbers, 11
Comments, 21-22
Compare-and-exchange pass, 155
compareandprocess (procedure), 206
Compilers, 8
Components, of array, 122
Component type, 122
Compound statement, 22
    use with **for** statement, 60-61
Computer, 1-9

Computer hardware, 4-6
Computer software, 6-9
Computer terminals, 5
Condition, 48-49
const, 42
Constant definitions, 41-42
Constants, 10
    Boolean, 14
    character, 15
    integer, 10, 11
    real, 11-14
    string, 15
    user defined, 41-42
Constructors, set, 216-217
Counter, 36
Counting, 36-37
CPU, 5

D

Data, 2
Data processing, 2
Data type definitions, 111ff.
Data types, 10-15
    pointer, 110, 187-196
    scalar, 110-118
    simple, 110-120
    standard, 11, 20, 110
    structured, 110
    subrange, 110, 118-120
date (record), 178
day (data type), 112ff., 124
day (record), 178
dealer (program), 77-78
Declarations
    assumed, 31
    function, 88-89
    procedure, 93-94
    set, 215-216
    variable, 29-32
Declarations and definitions, order of, 111
Definitions
    data type, 111ff.
    record, 175ff.
delete (procedure), 195
Deletion, from linked list, 194-195
Designator, function, 54
diagonal (function), 105
diagonal (program), 57
Diagrams, for indicating scopes of identifiers, 98-102
Difference, of sets, 217-218
Dimensions, of arrays, 139

Direct access, 6
Direct access files, 199
dispose (standard procedure), 188
div, 24, 25
Dividing-line value, in Quicksort, 162ff.
do, 59ff.
Dot, in field designator, 176
downto, 60
Dynamic variables, 186-187

E

E (in floating point notation), 12-13
Elements
    of array, 122 (footnote)
    of set, 213
Eliminating recursion, 167-173
else, 73ff.
else if, 82
employee (record), 177
end, 22
    use with **for** statement, 60-61
eof (standard predicate), 66-67, 201ff.
eoln (standard predicate), 66, 211ff.
error (procedure), 208
Exponent, 12
Exponential notation, 12-13
Expressions, 23-24, 44-58
    Boolean, 48-54
    containing sets, 217-219
    evaluation of, 45-48, 53, 55, 57
    variables in, 34-37
    with more than one operator, 44-48
External files, 200
External sorting, 154
extremes (procedure), 127

F

Factorial, 92-93, 105-108
    recursive definition of, 105-108
factorial (function), 92, 107
    recursive version, 107
false (Boolean constant), 14
Field designator, 176
    compared with indexed variable, 177
Field indentifiers, 175ff.
    scopes of, 184-186
Field, of record, 175ff.
field (program), 48
field1 (program), 63
fields (program), 62
fields2 (program), 64

Field-width parameters, 17-20
File-handling procedures, 200-203
Files, 199-214
    direct access, 199
    external, 200
    local, 200
    random, 199
    sequential, 199-214
    text, 210-213
File-update problem, 204-210
fileupdate (program), 208-210
File window, 199ff.
find (procedure), 195
Fixed part, 183
Flag, 220
Floating-point notation, 12-13
for, 59-65
for statements
    and arrays, 125-126, 139ff.
    scalar data types in, 117
Formal parameters, 89ff.
    scope rules for, 101-102
FORTRAN, 8
fracdemo (program), 91
frac (function), 89
fraction (record), 178
function, 89
Function declaration, 88-89
Function designator, 54
Function header, 89, 91
Function name
    assignment of value-to-be-returned
        to, 90, 93
    scope rules for, 101-102
Functions, 88-93, 96-109
    on scalar data types, 112-117
    standard, 54-57

G

game (program), 104-105
Gap, in Shellsort, 160-162
Generator, pseudorandom number,
    103-105
getdata (procedure), 141-145
getname (procedure), 135
get (standard procedure), 200, 201
Global variables, 99, 102-105
goto, 227-231
grade (data type), 112ff.
grades (program), 83
grades1 (program), 85

Guessing game, program to play, 104-105
Guide words, 152

H

Hardware, computer, 4-6
Hardware version of Pascal, 22-23
Header record, 189ff.
Heading
    function, 89, 91
    procedure, 94
    program, 20-21
Higher-level languages, 8-9

I

if, 72ff.
if statements
    indentation of, 80
    in multiway selection, 80-83
    in one-way selection, 72-73
    in two-way selection, 73-74
    nested, 78-80
in, 218-219
Index
    array, 121ff.
    table to aid in searching, 152-154
Indexed variable, 123
    compared with field designator, 177
Index type, 122
Information, 1-2
Information processing, 2
Indentation
    of compound statements, 22
    of for statements, 60-61
    of nested if statements, 80
Input, 37-39
    of arrays, 129-130
input (standard file), 21, 213
Input devices, 4, 5
insert (function), 192-193
Insertion, into linked list, 193
Integer constants, 10
integer (data types), 10, 11
Integers, printing, 16-18
Interactive programs, 40-41
Internal sorting, 154
Interpreters, 8-9
Intersection, of sets, 217-218

K

Knowledge, and information, 1-2

L

Language processors, 8, 9
Letter grades, computing, 82-83
Limitations, on sets, 216
Line separator character, 210ff.
Linked list, 189ff.
Link field, 189ff.
List
    linked, 189ff.
    one-dimensional array as, 121
List processing, 189-196
Local files, 200
Locations, memory, 4-5

M

Machine language, 7
Magnetic disk, 6
Magnetic tape, 6
Main memory, using, 28-43
Mask, 221
Master file, 204ff.
master (record), 204
Median, 164
Memory
    auxiliary, 4, 6
    main, 4-5, 28ff.
merit (program), 73
Microprocessor, 5
mod, 24, 25
Modules, 88
month (data type), 112ff.
Multidimensional arrays, 138-145
Multiway selection, 78-86

N

Nesting
    of for statements, 141ff.
    of parentheses, 47
    of records, 178-182
New master file, 204ff.
new (standard procedure), 188
nextmaster (procedure), 207
nil, 189
not, 52
Numbers, pseudorandom, 103-105

O

odd (standard predicate), 66
officer (data type), 112ff.
Old master file, 204ff.
One-dimensional arrays, 121-138
   applications of, 125ff.
One-way glass analogy, for scopes of
   identifiers, 98-99
One-way selection, 72-73
Operand, 24
Operating system, 9
Operator priorities, 45ff.
Operators
   arithmetic, 24ff.
   Boolean, 52-54
   on scalar data types, 112-117
   on sets, 216-219
   relational, 49-51
or, 52
Order
   of definitions and declarations, 111
   of values in scalar data types, 112-
   114
Ordinal numbers, 114-117
ord (standard function), 114-117
Output, of arrays, 129-130
Output devices, 4, 5
output (standard file), 20-21, 213

P

pack (standard procedure), 131-132
Packed arrays, 131-135
   of characters, 132-135
Parameters
   actual, 54ff.
   field-width, 17-20
   formal, 89
   value, 94
   variable, 94-95
Parentheses
   in expressions, 46-48
   nested, 47
   used to enclose record variant, 182-
   184
Pascal, 1, 8, 10ff.
   hardware version of, 22-23
   publication version of, 22-23
Pascal machine, 9
Pass, compare and exchange, 155
passenger (record), 178
payroll (program), 67

payroll1 (program), 68
payroll2 (program), 74
payroll3 (program), 134-135
Perimeter, calculation of, 47-48
Period, in field designator, 176
person (record), 180
PL/I, 8
Pointer, 187ff.
Pointer data types, 110, 187-196
Political poll, processing data from,
   139-145
Predicates, 66-67, 211-213
pred (standard function), 113-114
prices (program), 149
Printers, high-speed, 5
printfac (program), 97
Printing Boolean values, 19
Printing characters and strings, 19-20
Printing integers, 16-18
Printing real numbers, 18
printvol (procedure), 93
Priorities
   of arithmetic operators, 45ff.
   of Boolean operators, 52
   of relational operations, 51, 218
   of set operators, 218
procedure, 93-94
Procedure heading, 94
Procedure name, 94
   scope rules for, 101-102
Procedures, 93-109
   file handling, 200-203
Procedure statement, 94
Program, 1
program, 20
Program heading, 20-21
Programmer, 1
Programming, 1
Programming languages, 1, 7-9
Programs
   interactive, 40-41
   Pascal, 20-23
Prompts, 40-41
Pseudorandom number generator,
   103-105
Pseudorandom numbers, 103-105
Publication version of Pascal, 22-23
put (standard procedure), 202-203
putdata (procedure), 143

Q

Quicksort, 155, 162-173
Quicksort (procedure), 166, 167

Quicksrt (procedure), 168
Quiksort (procedure), 171, 172-173
Quotient, 24, 25

R

Random access, 6
Random files, 199
random (function), 104
rank (data type), 112ff.
readclass (procedure), 190
read (statement), 37-39, 211-213
readln (statement), 37-39, 211-213
Real constants, 11-14
Real numbers, printing, 18
real (standard data type), 11-14
Record assignment, 177
Record definitions, 175-178
Records, 175-198
    nested, 178-182
Record variants, 182-184
Recursion, 105-108
    eliminating, 167-173
    in Quicksort, 164ff.
    use in designing nonrecursive
        procedures, 173
    when to use, 108
reference (record), 182, 183, 184
Refinement, stepwise, 76
Relational operators, 49-51
    for sets, 218-219
    priorities of, 51, 218
Remainder, 24, 25
repeat, 68-70
    distinguished from **while**, 69-70
Repetition, 59-71
reset (standard procedure), 200-201
rewrite (standard procedure), 203
Rounding, 56-57
round (standard function), 56-57
Rows, of two-dimensional arrays, 139

S

Sales tax, computation of, 39-41, 42
Scalar data types, 110-118
    as index types, 124-125
    in **for** and **case** statements, 117-118
    operators and functions on, 112-117
    order of values for, 112-114
    user defined, 112
Scanner, 222-223

scan (program), 223
Scopes
    of field identifiers, 184-187
    of identifiers, 96-102
Searching, 146-154
    of linked lists, 195-196
Search
    binary, 150-154
    sequential, 146-149
Seed, 103-105
Selection, 72-87
    multiway, 78-86
    one-way, 72-73
    two-way, 73-78
Selector, 84
Semicolon
    for separating statements, 16
    with **for** statement, 61
Sentinel, 67-68
    in sequential search, 147
Sequential access, 6
Sequential files, 199-214
Sequential search, 146-149
Set constructors, 216-217
Set declarations, 215-216
Sets, 215-223
    applications of, 219-223
    limitations on, 216
    operations on, 216-219
Shellsort, 155, 160-162
Shellsort (procedure), 161
Simple data types, 110-120
Soft count (in blackjack), 75
Sorting, 146, 154-174
    external, 154
    internal, 154
Sorting techniques
    Bubblesort, 155-160
    Quicksort, 155, 162-173
    Shellsort, 155, 160-162
sqr (standard function), 54-57
sqrt (standard function), 56
Square, of number, 54
Stack, 169-170, 171ff.
Standard data types, 11, 30, 110
Standard functions, 54-57
Standard procedures
    file-handling, 200-203
    for textfiles, 211-213
Statements, 15
Static variables, 187
Stepwise refinement, 76
String constants, 15

Strings
    as packed arrays of characters,
        132-135
    printing, 19-20
Structured data types, 110
    arrays, 121-145
    files, 199-214
    records, 175-198
    sets, 215-223
student (record), 189
Sublists, in Quicksort, 162ff.
Subrange data types, 110, 118-120
Subset, 218-219
succ (standard function), 113-114
Superset, 218-219
Symbols, 222
System software, 6-7

T

Tables
    translation, 130-131
    two-dimensional arrays as, 139
Tag field, 183
tax (program), 40
tax1 (program), 41
tax2 (program), 42
Telephone directory, used to illustrate
        binary search, 149-150
Textfiles, 210-213
    standard procedures for, 211-213
then, 72ff.
Three-dimensional array, 139
Thumb index, of dictionary, 152
to, 60
Top, of stack, 169, 170
Transaction file, 204ff.
Translation tables, 130-131
Translators, 8-9
trans (record), 204
transtype (data type), 204
Time sharing, 9
Truncation, 56-57
trunc (standard function), 56-57
Two dimensional arrays, 138-145
    applications of, 139-145
Two-way selection, 73-78
type, 111
Type (*see also* Data type)
    component, 122
    index, 122

U

Union, of sets, 217-218
unpack (standard procedure), 131-132
until, 68-70
Update, of sequential files, 204-210
updateordelete (procedure), 207
Upward arrow
    in buffer variable, 200
    in pointer types and variables, 187ff.
User-defined scalar types, 112

V

Value
    dividing-line, 162ff.
    of variable, 29
Value parameters, 94
Values, 10
var, 30-32
    used to declare variable parameters,
        95
Variable name, 29
Variable parameters, 94-95
Variables, 28ff.
    array, 123, 125
    buffer, 200
    dynamic, 187
    global, 99, 102-105
    indexed, 123
    in expressions, 34-37
    local, 102
    scope rules for, 96-102
    static, 186
Variant part, 182
Variants, record, 182-184
vol (function), 91
volumes (program), 96

W

weather (record), 175
while, 65-68
    distinguished from **repeat**, 69-70
Window, file, 199ff.
with, 180ff.
writeln (statement), 15-20, 211-213
write (statement), 15-20, 211-213

```pascal
Program       (input, output);
    { raises m to the nth power }

    VAR
        answer: char;
        x, y: integer;

    Function power ( m, n: integer ): integer;
    BEGIN

        If n = 0 Then
        power := 1

        ELSE
        power := m * power (m, n-1)
    END;  {of power}


    BEGIN

        REPEAT
            writeln ('Enter number and power');
            readln (x, y);
            writeln (power (x, y));
            writeln ('Do you want to try another?');
            write ('Answer Y (yes) or N (no):
            readln (answer)
        Until   answer <> 'Y';
            writeln ('Have a good day')

    END.
```